FAVORITE BRAND NAME

Best-Loved

CHOCOLATE RECIPES

PUBLICATIONS INTERNATIONAL, LTD.

Front cover photography: Peter Dean Ross Photographs, Chicago

Pictured on the front cover *(clockwise from top left):* Bittersweet Chocolate Pound Cake *(page 206),* Truffles *(page 360),* Chocolate Petits Fours *(page 216)* and Triple Layer Cheesecake *(page 236).*

Pictured on the back cover *(clockwise from top):* Chocolate Strawberry Shortcake *(page 156),* Chocolate Mayonnaise Cake *(page 160),* Chocolate Fudge Cookie Cakes *(page 68)* and Chocolate Festival Cheesecake *(page 230).*

Microwave Cooking: Microwave ovens vary in wattage. The microwave cooking times given in this publication are approximate. Use the cooking times as guidelines and check for doneness before adding more time. Consult manufacturer's instructions for suitable microwave-safe cooking dishes.

Contents

Where Chocolate Dreams Begin

A day without the sweet indulgence of deep, dark chocolate is a day incomplete! Once chocolate was introduced to the American colonies in 1693 as a rich and creamy beverage, this decadent worldly delight swept the country—Americans everywhere were crazed by this velvety smooth sensation. As its fame as an irresistible beverage continued to grow, the desire to consume chocolate in other forms was overwhelming. And so the trials and testing began. In 1911 the first candy bar, a perfect combination of the much sought-after chocolate taste and ready-to-eat convenience, was introduced to America. But that's not the end of it. In the 1930's, a clever woman broke one of those ever-popular solid chocolate bars into pieces and threw them into her ordinary cookie dough. Thus, chocolate chips were born. Through the years, this luxurious treat has become more than just a simple chocolatey beverage, melt-in-your-mouth candy bar, or warm and gooey chips in cookies. It has become a true classic loved by many in its numerous forms and varieties.

Carry on a tradition that began in America over 200 years ago and create your own chocolate fantasies. With ten marvelous chapters packed with memorable treasures of breads, cookies, cakes, candies and more, the possibilities are endless. To help you achieve chocolate perfection every time, the following guidelines are chock-full of tips and hints for successful baking and candy making. Be sure to read this section before you begin your journey into the magical world of chocolate.

GENERAL GUIDELINES

Take the guess work out of baking by practicing the following techniques:

◾ Read the entire recipe before beginning to be sure you have all the necessary ingredients and utensils.

◾ Remove butter, margarine and cream cheese from the refrigerator to soften, if necessary.

◾ Toast, chop and grind nuts, peel and slice fruit, and melt chocolate before preparing the recipe.

◾ Measure all the ingredients accurately and assemble them in the order they are listed in the recipe.

◾ Be sure to use the pan size specified in the recipe. Prepare the pans according to the recipe directions.

◾ Adjust oven racks and preheat the oven. Check the oven temperature for accuracy with an oven thermometer.

◾ Follow recipe directions and baking times exactly. Check for doneness using the test given in the recipe.

MELTING CHOCOLATE

Make sure the utensils used for melting chocolate are completely dry. Moisture causes the chocolate to "seize," meaning, it becomes stiff and grainy. If this happens, add ½ teaspoon shortening (not butter) for each ounce of chocolate and stir until smooth. Chocolate scorches easily, and once scorched cannot be used. Follow one of these three methods for successful melting:

Double Boiler: This is the safest method because it prevents scorching. Place the chocolate in the top of a double boiler or in a heatproof bowl over hot, not boiling, water; stir chocolate until smooth. (Make sure that the water remains just below a simmer and is one inch below the bottom of the top pan). Be careful that no steam or water gets into the chocolate.

Direct Heat: Place the chocolate in a heavy saucepan and melt over very low heat, stirring constantly. Remove the chocolate from heat as soon as it is melted. Be sure to watch the chocolate carefully because it is easily scorched when using this method.

Microwave Oven: Place an unwrapped 1-ounce square or 1 cup of chips in small microwavable bowl. Microwave on HIGH 1 to 1½ minutes, stirring after 1 minute. Stir the chocolate at 30 second intervals until smooth. Be sure to stir microwaved chocolate since it may retain its original shape even when melted.

STORING

Chocolate: Since both heat and moisture adversely affect chocolate, it should be stored at room temperature wrapped in foil or waxed paper, but not plastic wrap. Bittersweet and semisweet chocolate can be stored a very long time, as long as ten years. Because they contain milk solids, white chocolate and milk chocolate have a much shorter shelf life and should be used within about 9 months.

Cookies, bar cookies and brownies: Unbaked cookie dough can be refrigerated for up to 1 week or frozen for up to 6 weeks. Rolls of dough should be sealed tightly in plastic wrap; other doughs should be stored in airtight containers. Label dough or container with baking information for convenience.

Store soft and crisp cookies separately at room temperature to prevent changes in texture and flavor. Keep soft cookies in airtight containers. If they begin to dry out, add a piece of apple or bread to the container to help them retain moisture. Store crisp cookies in containers with loose-fitting lids to prevent moisture buildup. If they become soggy, heat undecorated cookies in a 300°F oven for 3 to 5 minutes.

Store cookies with sticky glazes, fragile decorations and icing in a single layer between sheets of waxed paper. As a rule, crisp cookies freeze better than soft , moist cookies. Rich, buttery bar cookies and brownies are an exception to this rule since they freeze extremely well. Freeze baked cookies in airtight containers or freezer bags for up to 6 months. Thaw cookies and brownies unwrapped at room temperature.

Cakes and cheesecakes: Store one-layer cakes in their baking pans, tightly covered. Store two- or three-layer cakes in a cake-saver or under a large inverted bowl. If the cake has a fluffy or cooked frosting, insert a teaspoon handle under the edge of the cover to prevent an airtight seal and moisture buildup. Cakes with whipped cream frostings or cream fillings and cheesecakes should be stored in the refrigerator.

Unfrosted cakes can be frozen for up to 4 months if well wrapped in plastic. Thaw in their wrapping at room temperature. Frosted cakes should be frozen unwrapped until the frosting hardens, and then wrapped and sealed; freeze for up to 2 months. To thaw, remove the wrapping and thaw at room temperature or in the refrigerator. Cheesecakes can be refrigerated for up to 1 week. Cakes with fruit or custard fillings and cheesecakes do not freeze well as a they become soggy when thawed.

Candy: Store candy between sheets of waxed paper or plastic wrap in an airtight container in a cool, dry place. Store hard candies and soft candies separately to prevent changes in texture and flavor. When stored properly, most candy will keep up to 2 to 3 weeks. Candies like fudge and caramels can be wrapped airtight and frozen for up to 1 year. Thaw candy unwrapped at room temperature for 3 hours.

FOR CHOCOLATE LOVERS EVERYWHERE, THIS BOOK'S FOR YOU!

1½ cups all-purpose flour

½ cup sugar

1½ teaspoons CALUMET® Baking
   Powder

½ teaspoon cinnamon

¼ teaspoon salt

2 eggs, lightly beaten

½ cup milk

½ cup sour cream or plain
   yogurt

¼ cup (½ stick) margarine,
   melted

1 teaspoon vanilla

1 package (4 ounces) BAKER'S®
   GERMAN'S® Sweet
   Chocolate, chopped

CHOCOLATE CHUNK SOUR CREAM MUFFINS

Makes 12 muffins

HEAT oven to 375°F.

MIX flour, sugar, baking powder, cinnamon and salt; set aside. Stir eggs, milk, sour cream, margarine and vanilla in large bowl until well blended. Add flour mixture; stir until just moistened. Stir in chocolate.

FILL 12 paper- or foil-lined muffin cups ⅔ full with batter.

BAKE for 30 minutes or until toothpick inserted into center comes out clean. Remove from pan to cool on wire rack.

PREP TIME: 15 MINUTES

BAKE TIME: 30 MINUTES

From left to right: Chocolate Chunk Sour Cream Muffins and Chocolate Chunk Banana Bread (page 22)

German Chocolate Topping
(recipe follows)
1 package (18.25 ounces)
pudding-included German
chocolate cake mix

GERMAN CHOCOLATE MUFFINS

Makes 12 jumbo muffins

Preheat oven to 400°F. Grease 12 (3½-inch) large muffin cups; set aside. Prepare German Chocolate Topping; set aside.

Prepare cake mix according to package directions, *reducing* water by ¼ cup. Spoon into prepared muffin cups, filling half full. Sprinkle German Chocolate Topping evenly over tops of muffins.

Bake 20 to 25 minutes or until wooden pick inserted in center comes out clean. Cool in pan on wire rack 5 minutes. Remove from pan. Cool on wire rack 10 minutes. Serve warm or cool completely.

GERMAN CHOCOLATE TOPPING: Combine 3 tablespoons *each* chopped pecans, flaked coconut and packed brown sugar in small bowl until well blended.

German Chocolate Muffins

1¼ cups all-purpose flour
½ cup whole-wheat flour
¾ cup packed light brown sugar
¼ cup HERSHEY'S Cocoa
1 tablespoon baking powder
½ teaspoon baking soda
½ teaspoon salt
¼ teaspoon ground cinnamon
⅛ teaspoon ground nutmeg
1 cup chunky applesauce
⅓ cup butter or margarine,
   melted
¼ cup milk
1 egg
¾ cup raisins
Cinnamon Butter (recipe
   follows)

COCOA APPLESAUCE RAISIN MUFFINS

Makes about 15 muffins

Heat oven to 400°F. Grease bottoms of or line muffin cups (2½ inches in diameter) with paper bake cups. In large bowl, stir together all-purpose flour, whole-wheat flour, brown sugar, cocoa, baking powder, baking soda, salt, cinnamon and nutmeg. In small bowl, stir together applesauce, butter, milk and egg until well blended. Add to dry ingredients; stir just until dry ingredients are moistened. Stir in raisins. Fill muffin cups about ¾ full with batter. Bake 20 to 22 minutes or until wooden pick inserted in center comes out clean. Remove from pans to wire racks. Cool slightly. Meanwhile, prepare Cinnamon Butter. Serve with warm muffins.

CINNAMON BUTTER

½ cup (1 stick) butter or margarine, softened
2 tablespoons powdered sugar
⅛ to ¼ teaspoon ground cinnamon

In small bowl, beat butter, powdered sugar and cinnamon until well blended.

1¾ cups all-purpose flour

½ cup sugar

1 tablespoon DAVIS® Baking Powder

½ teaspoon salt

¾ cup milk

⅓ cup sour cream

1 egg

¼ cup FLEISCHMANN'S® Margarine, melted

20 OREO® Chocolate Sandwich Cookies, coarsely chopped

OREO® MUFFINS

Makes 1 dozen muffins

In medium bowl, combine flour, sugar, baking powder and salt; set aside.

In small bowl, combine milk, sour cream and egg; stir into flour mixture with margarine until just blended. Gently stir in cookies. Spoon batter into 12 greased 2½-inch muffin-pan cups.

Bake at 400°F for 20 to 25 minutes or until toothpick inserted in center comes out clean. Remove from pan; cool on wire rack. Serve warm or cold.

CHOCOLATE TIP

When Hernando Cortés, a Spanish general, landed on the shores of Mexico in 1519, the Aztecs honored him with a great banquet in the belief he was the reincarnation of one of their long lost Gods. At this sumptuous banquet, the Emperor Montezuma served xocoatl, a chocolate drink. It was not until 9 years later that Cortés was able to bring the cocoa bean back to his homeland. When this decadent flavor was introduced in Europe, a new taste sensation was born.

4 cups all-purpose flour

⅓ cup granulated sugar

2 tablespoons baking powder

½ teaspoon salt

½ cup cold butter, cut up

1 cup (half of 12-ounce package) NESTLÉ® TOLL HOUSE® Semi-Sweet Chocolate Mini Morsels

4 eggs, divided

1 cup CARNATION® Evaporated Milk

1½ teaspoons vanilla extract

2 tablespoons milk

MINI MORSEL TEA BISCUITS

Makes 18 biscuits

COMBINE flour, sugar, baking powder and salt in large bowl. With pastry blender or two knives, cut in butter until mixture resembles coarse crumbs. Stir in morsels.

BEAT 3 eggs, evaporated milk and vanilla in medium bowl. Add to flour mixture all at once; stir with fork to form a soft dough. Turn dough onto well-floured suface. Knead 6 to 8 times. Pat dough to ¾-inch thickness. Cut with floured 2½-inch biscuit cutter. Transfer to lightly greased baking sheets. Beat *remaining* egg and milk in small bowl; brush over biscuits.

BAKE in preheated 400°F oven for 14 to 16 minutes or until golden brown. Remove to wire racks; serve warm.

Mini Morsel Tea Biscuits

¾ cup plus 2 tablespoons
 all-purpose flour
¼ cup granulated sugar
2 tablespoons unsweetened
 cocoa powder
¼ teaspoon salt
4 eggs
1 cup milk
2 tablespoons butter or
 margarine, melted
½ teaspoon vanilla
 Powdered sugar

CHOCOLATE POPOVERS

Makes 6 popovers

1. Position rack in lower third of oven. Preheat oven to 375°F. Grease 6-cup popover pan or 6 (6-ounce) custard cups. Set custard cups in jelly-roll pan for easier handling.

2. Sift flour, granulated sugar, cocoa and salt into medium bowl; set aside.

3. Beat eggs in large bowl with electric mixer at low speed 1 minute. Beat in milk, butter and vanilla. Beat in flour mixture until smooth. Pour batter into prepared pan. Bake 50 minutes. Immediately remove popovers to wire rack. Generously sprinkle powdered sugar over popovers. Serve immediately.

Chocolate Popovers

⅔ cup sugar

⅓ cup Prune Purée (recipe follows) or prepared prune butter

2 egg whites

¼ cup semisweet miniature chocolate chips, melted

½ cup nonfat milk

1 teaspoon vanilla

1⅓ cups all-purpose flour

½ teaspoon baking powder

½ teaspoon salt

¼ teaspoon baking soda

⅓ cup semisweet miniature chocolate chips

CHOCOLATE–CHOCOLATE CHIP BREAD

Makes 1 loaf (12 slices)

Preheat oven to 350°F. Coat 8½×4½×2¾-inch loaf pan with vegetable cooking spray. In large bowl, beat sugar, prune purée, egg whites and melted chocolate chips until well blended. Mix in milk and vanilla. In medium bowl, combine flour, baking powder, salt and baking soda; stir into sugar mixture just until blended. Stir in chocolate chips. Spoon batter into prepared pan. Bake in center of oven 40 to 45 minutes until springy to the touch and wooden pick inserted in center comes out clean. Cool in pan 5 minutes; remove from pan to wire rack. Cool completely before slicing.

PRUNE PURÉE: Combine 1⅓ cups (8 ounces) pitted prunes and 6 tablespoons hot water in container of food processor or blender. Pulse on and off until prunes are finely chopped and smooth. Store leftovers in a covered container in the refrigerator for up to two months.

Chocolate–Chocolate Chip Bread

½ cup skim milk

½ cup plain nonfat yogurt

⅓ cup sugar

¼ cup orange juice

1 egg, slightly beaten

1 tablespoon freshly grated
orange peel

3 cups all-purpose biscuit
baking mix

½ cup HERSHEY'S MINI
CHIPS® Semi-Sweet
Chocolate

ORANGE CHOCOLATE CHIP BREAD

Makes 1 loaf (16 slices)

Heat oven to 350°F. Grease 9×5×3-inch loaf pan or spray with vegetable cooking spray. In large bowl, stir together milk, yogurt, sugar, orange juice, egg and orange peel; add baking mix. With spoon, beat until well blended, about 1 minute. Stir in small chocolate chips. Pour into prepared pan.

Bake 45 to 50 minutes or until wooden pick inserted in center comes out clean. Cool 10 minutes; remove from pan to wire rack. Cool completely before slicing. Garnish as desired. Wrap leftover bread in foil or plastic wrap. Store at room temperature or freeze for longer storage.

Orange Chocolate Chip Bread

2¼ cups all-purpose flour

1 teaspoon baking soda

¼ teaspoon salt

1 cup (2 sticks) margarine or
   butter, softened

2 cups sugar

5 eggs

3 squares BAKER'S®
   Unsweetened Chocolate,
   melted, cooled slightly

1 cup buttermilk or sour milk*

2 teaspoons vanilla

1 cup finely chopped nuts
   Powdered sugar (optional)
   Chopped nuts (optional)

*To make sour milk, add 1 tablespoon
vinegar to 1 cup milk; let stand
5 minutes.

CHOCOLATE NUT LOAVES

Makes 5 loaves

HEAT oven to 350°F.

MIX flour, baking soda and salt; set aside. Beat margarine and sugar in large bowl until light and fluffy. Add eggs, one at a time, beating well after each addition. Stir in chocolate.

ADD flour mixture alternately with buttermilk, beating after each addition until smooth. Mix in vanilla and 1 cup nuts. Pour into 5 greased and floured 5×3-inch loaf pans.

BAKE about 50 minutes or until toothpick inserted into centers comes out clean. Cool in pans 10 minutes. Remove from pans to cool on wire racks. Sprinkle with powdered sugar; garnish with chopped nuts, if desired.

PREP TIME: 30 MINUTES
BAKE TIME: 50 MINUTES

TIP: Loaves may also be baked in 2 (9×5-inch) loaf pans. Bake 1 hour.

From top to bottom: Chocolate Nut Loaf and
Chocolate Chunk Coffee Cake (page 23)

2 eggs, lightly beaten

1 cup mashed ripe bananas
(about 3 medium bananas)

⅓ cup vegetable oil

¼ cup milk

2 cups all-purpose flour

1 cup sugar

2 teaspoons CALUMET® Baking
Powder

¼ teaspoon salt

1 package (4 ounces) BAKER'S®
GERMAN'S® Sweet
Chocolate, coarsely
chopped

½ cup chopped nuts

CHOCOLATE CHUNK BANANA BREAD

Makes 1 loaf

HEAT oven to 350°F.

STIR eggs, bananas, oil and milk until well blended. Add flour, sugar, baking powder and salt; stir until just moistened. Stir in chocolate and nuts. Pour into greased 9×5-inch loaf pan.

BAKE for 55 minutes or until toothpick inserted into center comes out clean. Cool in pan 10 minutes. Remove from pan to cool on wire rack.

PREP TIME: 20 MINUTES
BAKE TIME: 55 MINUTES

CHOCOLATE TIP

BAKER'S® German's® Sweet Chocolate was created by Samuel German in 1852 as a quality snack-type chocolate bar. This unique formula is a special blend of chocolate, enriched with cocoa butter and sugar, and is the basis of a chocolate that retains its rich and mild flavor in recipes.

NUT LAYER:

- 1 package (4 ounces) BAKER'S® GERMAN'S® Sweet Chocolate, chopped
- ½ cup chopped nuts
- ¼ cup sugar
- 1 teaspoon cinnamon

CAKE:

- 1¾ cups all-purpose flour
- ½ teaspoon CALUMET® Baking Powder
- ¼ teaspoon salt
- 1 cup (½ pint) sour cream or plain yogurt
- 1 teaspoon baking soda
- ½ cup (1 stick) margarine or butter, softened
- 1 cup sugar
- 2 eggs
- ½ teaspoon vanilla

CHOCOLATE CHUNK COFFEE CAKE

Makes 9 servings

Heat oven to 350°F.

Mix chocolate, nuts, ¼ cup sugar and cinnamon; set aside. Mix flour, baking powder and salt; set aside. Combine sour cream and baking soda; set aside.

Beat margarine and 1 cup sugar in large bowl until light and fluffy. Add eggs, one at a time, beating well after each addition. Add vanilla. Add flour mixture alternately with sour cream mixture, beginning and ending with flour mixture. Spoon ½ the batter into greased 9-inch square pan. Top with ½ the chocolate-nut mixture, spreading carefully with spatula. Repeat layers.

Bake for 30 to 35 minutes or until cake begins to pull away from sides of pan. Cool in pan; cut into squares.

PREP TIME: 30 MINUTES
BAKE TIME: 30 TO 35 MINUTES

¾ cup butter or margarine,
   softened

1½ cups packed light brown sugar

 3 eggs

 2 teaspoons vanilla

 3 cups all-purpose flour

 2 teaspoons baking powder

 2 teaspoons ground cinnamon

1½ teaspoons baking soda

 ½ teaspoon ground nutmeg

 ¼ teaspoon salt

1½ cups dairy sour cream

 ½ cup semisweet chocolate chips

 ½ cup chopped walnuts
   Powdered sugar

SOUR CREAM COFFEE CAKE WITH CHOCOLATE AND WALNUTS

Makes one 10-inch coffee cake

Preheat oven to 350°F. Grease and flour 12-cup Bundt pan or 10-inch tube pan. Beat butter in large bowl with electric mixer on medium speed until creamy. Add brown sugar; beat until light and fluffy. Beat in eggs and vanilla until well blended. Combine flour, baking powder, cinnamon, baking soda, nutmeg and salt in large bowl; add to butter mixture alternately with sour cream. Beat on low speed, beginning and ending with flour mixture until well blended. Stir in chocolate chips and walnuts. Spoon into prepared pan.

Bake 45 to 50 minutes or until wooden toothpick inserted in center comes out clean. Cool in pan 15 minutes. Remove from pan to wire rack; cool completely. Store tightly covered at room temperature. Sprinkle with powdered sugar before serving.

Sour Cream Coffee Cake with Chocolate and Walnuts

Cocoa Streusel (recipe follows)

¾ **cup (1½ sticks) butter or margarine, softened**

1 **cup sugar**

3 **eggs**

1 **teaspoon vanilla extract**

½ **cup dairy sour cream**

3 **cups all-purpose flour**

2 **teaspoons baking powder**

1 **teaspoon baking soda**

1 **cup orange juice**

2 **teaspoons freshly grated orange peel**

½ **cup orange marmalade or apple jelly**

ORANGE STREUSEL COFFEECAKE

Makes 12 servings

Prepare Cocoa Streusel. Heat oven to 350°F. Generously grease 12-cup fluted tube pan or 10-inch tube pan. In large bowl, beat butter and sugar until creamy. Add eggs and vanilla; beat well. Add sour cream; beat until blended. Stir together flour, baking powder and baking soda; add alternately with orange juice to butter mixture, beating well after each addition. Stir in orange peel. Spread marmalade onto bottom of prepared pan; sprinkle half the streusel over marmalade. Carefully spread half the batter over streusel. Sprinkle remaining streusel over batter; spread remaining batter over streusel. Bake 1 hour to 1 hour 5 minutes or until wooden pick inserted in center comes out clean. With metal spatula, loosen cake from sides of pan; immediately invert onto serving plate. Serve warm or cool. Garnish as desired.

COCOA STREUSEL

⅔ **cup packed light brown sugar**

½ **cup chopped walnuts**

½ **cup MOUNDS® Sweetened Coconut Flakes (optional)**

¼ **cup HERSHEY'S Cocoa**

In small bowl, stir together brown sugar, walnuts, coconut, if desired and cocoa.

Orange Streusel Coffeecake

3 to 3½ cups all-purpose flour

3 tablespoons granulated sugar

1 package (¼ ounce) active dry
    yeast

1 teaspoon salt

1 cup plus 1 tablespoon milk,
    divided

3 tablespoons butter or
    margarine, at room
    temperature

1 egg, lightly beaten

1 milk chocolate candy bar
    (7 ounces), cut into
    16 pieces

2 teaspoons colored sugar

PETIT PAIN AU CHOCOLATE

Makes 8 rolls

1. Combine 3 cups flour, granulated sugar, yeast and salt in large bowl; set aside.

2. Combine 1 cup milk and butter in small saucepan. Heat over low heat until mixture is 120° to 130°F. (Butter does not need to completely melt.) Gradually stir milk mixture and egg into flour mixture to make soft dough that forms a ball. Turn out dough onto lightly floured surface; flatten slightly. Knead 8 to 10 minutes or until smooth and elastic, adding remaining ½ cup flour to prevent sticking if necessary.

3. Shape dough into a ball; place in large greased bowl. Turn dough over so that top is greased. Cover with towel; let rise in warm place about 1 hour or until doubled in bulk.

4. Punch down dough. Knead dough on lightly floured surface 1 minute. Roll dough, forming a loaf. Cut loaf into 8 pieces. Roll 1 dough piece into a 6-inch round. Place 2 pieces chocolate in center. Fold edges into center around chocolate. Place seam side down on lightly greased baking sheet. Repeat with remaining dough pieces. Place rolls 3 inches apart on baking sheet.

5. Cover rolls lightly with towel and let rise in warm place 20 to 30 minutes or until slightly puffed. Preheat oven to 400°F. Brush tops with remaining 1 tablespoon milk. Sprinkle with colored sugar. Bake 12 to 15 minutes or until rolls are golden brown. Serve immediately.

Petit Pain au Chocolate

1 BUTTER FLAVOR* CRISCO®
Stick or 1 cup BUTTER
FLAVOR CRISCO
all-vegetable shortening

1 cup packed brown sugar

1 cup granulated sugar

2 eggs

2 teaspoons vanilla

1⅔ cups all-purpose flour

1 teaspoon baking soda

1 teaspoon salt

½ teaspoon baking powder

3 cups quick oats (not instant or old fashioned), uncooked

1 baking bar (6 ounces) white chocolate, coarsely chopped

6 squares (1 ounce each) semisweet chocolate, coarsely chopped

½ cup coarsely chopped red candied cherries

½ cup sliced almonds

*Butter Flavor Crisco is artificially flavored.

BLACK FOREST OATMEAL FANCIES

Makes about 3 dozen cookies

1. **Heat** oven to 375°F. **Place** sheets of foil on countertop for cooling cookies.

2. **Combine** shortening, brown sugar, granulated sugar, eggs and vanilla in large bowl. **Beat** at medium speed of electric mixer until well blended.

3. **Combine** flour, baking soda, salt and baking powder. **Mix** into shortening mixture at low speed until well blended. **Stir** in, one at a time, oats, white chocolate, semisweet chocolate, cherries and nuts with spoon.

4. **Drop** rounded tablespoonfuls of dough 2 inches apart onto ungreased baking sheets.

5. **Bake** one baking sheet at a time at 375°F for 9 to 11 minutes or until set. *Do not overbake.* **Cool** 2 minutes on baking sheets. **Remove** cookies to foil to cool completely.

Black Forest Oatmeal Fancies

2½ cups all-purpose flour
1 teaspoon baking soda
½ teaspoon salt
1 cup butter or margarine,
 softened
1 cup packed light brown sugar
½ cup granulated sugar
2 eggs
1 tablespoon vanilla
1 cup semisweet chocolate chips
1 cup milk chocolate chips
1 cup vanilla milk chips
½ cup coarsely chopped pecans

ULTIMATE CHIPPERS

Makes about 6 dozen cookies

Preheat oven to 375°F. Combine flour, baking soda and salt in medium bowl.

Beat butter, brown sugar and granulated sugar in large bowl until light and fluffy. Beat in eggs and vanilla. Add flour mixture to butter mixture; beat until well blended. Stir in chips and pecans.

Drop by heaping teaspoonfuls 2 inches apart onto ungreased cookie sheets. Bake 10 to 12 minutes or until edges are golden brown. Let cookies stand on cookie sheets 2 minutes. Remove cookies to wire racks; cool completely.

1½ cups (3 sticks) butter, softened
1 cup granulated sugar
1 cup packed light brown sugar
3 eggs
2 teaspoons vanilla extract
3⅓ cups all-purpose flour
1½ teaspoons baking soda
¾ teaspoon salt
4 cups (24-ounce package)
 HERSHEY®S Semi-Sweet
 Chocolate Chips

HERSHEY®S MORE CHIPS CHOCOLATE CHIP COOKIES

Makes about 7½ dozen cookies

Preheat oven to 375°F. In large bowl, beat butter, granulated sugar and brown sugar until creamy. Add eggs and vanilla; beat until light and fluffy.

In another large bowl, stir together flour, baking soda and salt; gradually beat into butter mixture. Stir in chocolate chips. Drop by rounded teaspoonfuls onto ungreased cookie sheets.

Bake 8 to 10 minutes or until lightly browned. Cool slightly; remove from cookie sheets to wire racks. Cool completely.

Ultimate Chippers

1 BUTTER FLAVOR* CRISCO®
Stick or 1 cup BUTTER
FLAVOR CRISCO
all-vegetable shortening
1 cup packed brown sugar
½ cup granulated sugar
1 egg
½ cup sour cream
¼ cup warm honey
2 teaspoons vanilla
2½ cups all-purpose flour
1½ teaspoons baking powder
½ teaspoon salt
2 cups semisweet or milk
chocolate chips
1 cup coarsely chopped walnuts

*Butter Flavor Crisco is artificially
flavored.

SOUR CREAM CHOCOLATE CHIP COOKIES

Makes about 5 dozen cookies

1. **Heat** oven to 375°F. **Grease** baking sheets with shortening. **Place** sheets of foil on countertop for cooling cookies.

2. **Combine** shortening, brown sugar and granulated sugar in large bowl. **Beat** at medium speed of electric mixer until well blended. **Beat** in egg, sour cream, honey and vanilla. **Beat** until just blended.

3. **Combine** flour, baking powder and salt. **Mix** into shortening mixture at low speed until just blended. **Stir** in chocolate chips and nuts.

4. **Drop** slightly rounded measuring tablespoonfuls of dough 2 inches apart onto prepared baking sheets.

5. **Bake** one baking sheet at a time at 375°F for 10 to 12 minutes or until set. *Do not overbake.* **Cool** 2 minutes on baking sheets. **Remove** cookies to foil to cool completely.

Sour Cream Chocolate Chip Cookies

DOUBLY CHOCOLATE MINT COOKIES

Makes about 2½ dozen cookies

1 HERSHEY'S Cookies 'n' Mint
  Milk Chocolate Bar
  (7 ounces)
½ cup (1 stick) butter or
  margarine, softened
¾ cup sugar
1 egg
1 teaspoon vanilla extract
1 cup all-purpose flour
⅓ cup HERSHEY'S Cocoa
½ teaspoon baking soda
⅛ teaspoon salt
1 cup coarsely chopped nuts
  (optional)

Heat oven to 350°F. Cut chocolate bar into small pieces. In large mixer bowl, beat butter, sugar, egg and vanilla until light and fluffy. Combine flour, cocoa, baking soda and salt. Blend into butter mixture. Stir in chocolate and nuts, if desired. Drop rounded teaspoonfuls onto ungreased cookie sheet. Bake 10 to 12 minutes or until set. Cool slightly; remove to wire rack. Cool completely.

FORGOTTEN CHIPS COOKIES

Makes about 2½ dozen cookies

2 egg whites
⅛ teaspoon cream of tartar
⅛ teaspoon salt
⅔ cup sugar
1 teaspoon vanilla extract
1 cup HERSHEY'S Semi-Sweet
  Chocolate Chips or Milk
  Chocolate Chips

Heat oven to 375°F. Lightly grease cookie sheets. In small bowl, beat egg whites, cream of tartar and salt until soft peaks form. Gradually add sugar, beating until stiff peaks form. Carefully fold in vanilla extract and chocolate chips. Drop dough by teaspoonfuls onto prepared cookie sheets.

Place cookie sheets in preheated oven; immediately turn off oven and allow cookies to remain in oven six hours or overnight without opening door. Remove cookies from cookie sheets. Store in airtight container in cool, dry place.

1 cup Prune Purée (recipe
    follows) or prepared prune
    butter
¾ cup granulated sugar
¾ cup packed brown sugar
3 egg whites
1 teaspoon vanilla
2¼ cups all-purpose flour
1 teaspoon baking soda
1 teaspoon salt
2 cups (12 ounces) semisweet
    chocolate chips

LOW FAT CHOCOLATE CHIP COOKIES

Makes about 60 (2¼-inch) cookies

Preheat oven to 375°F. Coat baking sheets with vegetable cooking spray. In large bowl, beat prune purée, sugars, egg whites and vanilla until well blended. In small bowl, combine flour, baking soda and salt; mix into prune purée mixture until well blended. Stir in chocolate chips. Drop tablespoonfuls of dough onto prepared baking sheets, spacing 2 inches apart; flatten slightly. Bake in center of oven about 10 minutes until lightly browned around edges. Remove from baking sheets to wire racks to cool completely.

PRUNE PURÉE: Combine 1⅓ cups (8 ounces) pitted prunes and 6 tablespoons hot water in container of food processor or blender. Pulse on and off until prunes are finely chopped and smooth. Store leftovers in a covered container in the refrigerator for up to two months.

FAVORITE RECIPE FROM CALIFORNIA PRUNE BOARD

2¼ cups all-purpose flour
1 teaspoon baking soda
1 teaspoon salt
1 cup (2 sticks) butter, softened
¾ cup granulated sugar
¾ cup packed brown sugar
1 teaspoon vanilla extract
2 eggs
2 cups (12-ounce package)
    NESTLÉ® TOLL HOUSE®
    Semi-Sweet Chocolate
    Morsels
1 cup chopped nuts

ORIGINAL NESTLÉ® TOLL HOUSE® CHOCOLATE CHIP COOKIES

Makes about 5 dozen cookies

Combine flour, baking soda and salt in small bowl; set aside. Beat butter, granulated sugar, brown sugar and vanilla in large mixer bowl until creamy. Add eggs, one at a time, beating well after each addition; gradually beat in flour mixture. Stir in morsels and nuts. Drop by rounded measuring tablespoonfuls onto ungreased cookie sheets.

Bake in preheated 375°F oven for 9 to 11 minutes or until edges are golden brown. Let stand for 2 minutes; remove to wire racks to cool completely.

2 extra-ripe, medium DOLE®
    Bananas, peeled and cut
    into chunks
2 cups granola
1½ cups all-purpose flour
1 cup packed brown sugar
1 teaspoon baking powder
1 teaspoon ground cinnamon
2 eggs
½ cup margarine, melted
¼ cup vegetable oil
1 cup semisweet chocolate chips

SAN FRANCISCO COOKIES

Makes about 16 cookies

■ Preheat oven to 350°F. Lightly grease cookie sheets. In blender or food processor, process bananas until puréed (1 cup).

■ Combine granola, flour, sugar, baking powder and cinnamon in large bowl. Beat in puréed bananas, eggs, margarine and oil. Stir in chocolate chips.

■ Drop by ¼ cupfuls onto prepared cookie sheets. Spread dough into 2½- to 3-inch circles. Bake about 16 minutes or until golden. Remove to wire racks to cool.

Original Nestlé® Toll House® Chocolate Chip Cookies

1 ripe, medium banana
1¼ cups all-purpose flour
1 teaspoon baking powder
½ teaspoon salt
⅓ cup butter or margarine, softened
⅓ cup granulated sugar
⅓ cup firmly packed light brown sugar
1 large egg
1 teaspoon vanilla
1 cup milk chocolate chips
½ cup coarsely chopped walnuts (optional)

BANANA CHOCOLATE CHIP SOFTIES

Makes about 3 dozen cookies

1. Preheat oven to 375°F. Lightly grease cookie sheets.

2. Peel banana and place in small bowl. Mash enough banana with fork to measure ½ cup; set aside.

3. Place flour, baking powder and salt in small bowl; stir to combine. Beat butter, granulated sugar and brown sugar in large bowl with electric mixer at medium speed until light and fluffy. Beat in banana, egg and vanilla. Add flour mixture. Beat at low speed until well blended. Stir in chips and walnuts with mixing spoon. (Dough will be soft.)

4. Drop rounded teaspoonfuls of dough 2 inches apart onto prepared cookie sheets. Bake 9 to 11 minutes or until edges are golden brown. Let cookies stand on cookie sheets 2 minutes. Remove cookies with spatula to wire racks; cool completely.

5. Store tightly covered at room temperature. These cookies do not freeze well.

Banana Chocolate Chip Softies

1 package DUNCAN HINES®
  Chocolate Chip Cookie Mix
1 egg
⅓ cup CRISCO® Oil
3 tablespoons water
10 ounces chocolate-flavored
  candy coating
⅓ cup chopped sliced natural
  almonds

SPECIAL CHOCOLATE CHIP SANDWICHES

Makes 29 Sandwich Cookies

1. Preheat oven to 375°F.

2. Combine cookie mix, egg, oil and water in large bowl. Stir until thoroughly blended. Drop by rounded teaspoonfuls 2 inches apart onto ungreased baking sheets. Bake at 375°F for 8 to 10 minutes or until light golden brown. Cool 1 minute on baking sheets. Remove to cooling racks. Cool completely.

3. Place chocolate candy coating in small saucepan. Melt on low heat, stirring frequently until smooth.

4. To assemble, spread about ½ teaspoon melted coating on bottom of one cookie; top with second cookie. Press together to make sandwiches. Repeat with remaining cookies. Dip one-third of each sandwich cookie in remaining melted coating and sprinkle with chopped almonds. Place on cooling racks until coating is set. Store between layers of waxed paper in airtight container.

TIP: Place waxed paper under cooling racks to catch chocolate coating drips and to make clean-up easier.

Special Chocolate Chip Sandwiches

1 cup (2 sticks) margarine or
    butter, softened
¾ cup firmly packed brown
    sugar
¾ cup granulated sugar
1 teaspoon vanilla
2 eggs
2¼ cups all-purpose flour
1 teaspoon baking soda
¼ teaspoon salt
1 package (12 ounces)
    BAKER'S® Semi-Sweet Real
    Chocolate Chips
1 cup chopped nuts (optional)

BAKER'S® CHOCOLATE CHIP COOKIES

Makes about 6 dozen cookies

HEAT oven to 375°F.

BEAT margarine, brown sugar, granulated sugar, vanilla and eggs until light and fluffy. Mix in flour, baking soda and salt. Stir in chips and nuts. Drop by rounded teaspoonfuls, 2 inches apart, onto ungreased cookie sheets.

BAKE for 8 to 10 minutes or until golden brown. Remove from cookie sheets to cool on wire racks.

PREP TIME: 15 MINUTES
BAKE TIME: 8 TO 10 MINUTES

Baker's® Chocolate Chip Cookies

1 cup sugar

¼ cup Prune Purée (recipe follows) or prepared prune butter or 1 jar (2½ ounces) first-stage baby food prunes

¼ cup water

2 tablespoons nonfat milk

1 teaspoon vanilla

½ teaspoon instant espresso coffee powder or 1 teaspoon instant coffee granules

1 cup all-purpose flour

½ cup unsweetened cocoa powder

¾ teaspoon baking soda

½ teaspoon salt

½ cup dried sour cherries

¼ cup chopped walnuts

¼ cup semisweet chocolate chips

CHERRY CHOCOLATE CHIP WALNUT COOKIES

Makes 12 large cookies

Preheat oven to 350°F. Coat baking sheets with vegetable cooking spray. In large bowl, whisk together sugar, prune purée, water, milk, vanilla and espresso powder until mixture is well blended, about 1 minute. Combine flour, cocoa, baking soda and salt; mix into prune purée mixture until well blended. Stir in cherries, walnuts and chocolate chips. Spoon twelve equal mounds of dough onto prepared baking sheets, spacing at least 2 inches apart. Bake in center of oven 18 to 20 minutes or until set and tops of cookies feel dry to the touch. Cool on baking sheets 2 minutes; remove to wire rack to cool completely.

PRUNE PURÉE: Combine 1⅓ cups (8 ounces) pitted prunes and 6 tablespoons hot water in container of food processor or blender. Pulse on and off until prunes are finely chopped and smooth. Store leftovers in a covered container in the refrigerator for up to two months.

TIP: In chocolate baked goods using prune purée, the addition of coffee powder enhances the chocolate flavor.

FAVORITE RECIPE FROM **CALIFORNIA PRUNE BOARD**

Cherry Chocolate Chip Walnut Cookies

⅔ **BUTTER FLAVOR* CRISCO®
Stick or ⅔ cup BUTTER
FLAVOR CRISCO all-
vegetable shortening**

1 **cup sugar**

1 **egg**

½ **teaspoon strawberry extract**

½ **cup buttermilk****

6 **tablespoons puréed frozen
sweetened strawberries**

1¾ **cups all-purpose flour**

6 **tablespoons unsweetened
cocoa powder**

¾ **teaspoon baking soda**

½ **teaspoon salt**

1½ **cups white chocolate baking
chips or white chocolate
bar, cut into pieces**

*Butter Flavor Crisco is artificially
flavored*

**You may substitute 1½ teaspoons
lemon juice or vinegar plus enough
milk to make ½ cup for the
buttermilk. Stir. Wait 5 minutes
before using.*

IVORY CHIP STRAWBERRY FUDGE DROPS

Makes about 2½ dozen cookies

1. **Heat** oven to 350°F. **Grease** baking sheets with shortening. **Place** sheets of foil on countertop for cooling cookies.

2. **Combine** shortening, sugar, egg and strawberry extract in large bowl. **Beat** at medium speed of electric mixer until well blended. **Beat** in buttermilk and strawberry purée.

3. **Combine** flour, cocoa, baking soda and salt. **Mix** into shortening mixture at low speed of electric mixer until blended. **Stir** in white chocolate chips.

4. **Drop** by rounded tablespoonfuls 2 inches apart onto prepared baking sheets.

5. **Bake** one baking sheet at a time at 350°F for 11 to 12 minutes or until tops spring back when pressed lightly. *Do not overbake.* **Cool** 2 minutes on baking sheets. **Remove** cookies to foil to cool completely.

½ cup packed light brown sugar

⅓ cup Prune Purée (recipe follows) or prepared prune butter or 1 jar (2½ ounces) first-stage baby food prunes

¼ cup granulated sugar

2 tablespoons vegetable shortening

1 egg white

1 teaspoon vanilla

¾ cup all-purpose flour

½ teaspoon salt

½ teaspoon baking soda

1 cup rolled oats

⅔ cup semisweet chocolate chips

THE FIRST FAMILY'S CHOCOLATE CHIP OATMEAL COOKIES

Makes 24 (2½-inch) cookies

Preheat oven to 375°F. Coat baking sheets with vegetable cooking spray. In mixer bowl, beat brown sugar, prune purée, granulated sugar, shortening, egg white and vanilla at high speed 1 minute. Combine flour, salt and baking soda; stir into sugar mixture. Stir in rolled oats and chocolate chips. (Batter will be stiff.) Drop tablespoonfuls of dough onto prepared baking sheets, spacing 2 inches apart. Bake in center of oven about 10 minutes until golden brown. Cool on baking sheets 1 minute; remove to wire racks to cool completely.

PRUNE PURÉE: Combine 1⅓ cups (8 ounces) pitted prunes and 6 tablespoons hot water in container of food processor or blender. Pulse on and off until prunes are finely chopped and smooth. Store leftovers in a covered container in the refrigerator for up to two months.

FAVORITE RECIPE FROM CALIFORNIA PRUNE BOARD

1 package (18.25 ounces) devil's
    food chocolate cake mix
⅓ cup water
¼ cup butter or margarine,
    softened
1 large egg
1 cup large vanilla baking chips
½ cup coarsely chopped walnuts

QUICK CHOCOLATE SOFTIES

Makes about 2 dozen large or 4 dozen small cookies

1. Preheat oven to 350°F. Lightly grease cookie sheets.

2. Combine cake mix, water, butter and egg in large bowl. Beat with electric mixer at low speed until moistened. Increase speed to medium; beat 1 minute. (Dough will be thick.) Stir in chips and walnuts with mixing spoon until well blended.

3. Drop heaping *teaspoonfuls* of dough 2 inches apart (for smaller cookies) or heaping *tablespoonfuls* 3 inches apart (for larger cookies) onto prepared cookie sheets. Bake 10 to 12 minutes or until set. Let cookies stand on cookie sheets 1 minute. Remove cookies with spatula to wire racks; cool completely.

4. Store tightly covered at room temperature or freeze up to 3 months.

PREP TIME: 15 MINUTES

C H O C O L A T E   T I P

The word chocolate originated from the Aztec word xocoatl, meaning "bitter water"—an unexpected translation since chocolate is loved for its sweetness.

The Aztec word, however, described an ancient drink made from unsweetened cocoa beans and spices, which was probably rather bitter.

Quick Chocolate Softies

1 cup (2 sticks) margarine or
butter, softened
1¼ cups firmly packed brown
sugar
½ cup granulated sugar
2 eggs
2 tablespoons milk
2 teaspoons vanilla
1¾ cups all-purpose flour
1 teaspoon baking soda
½ teaspoon salt (optional)
2½ cups QUAKER® Oats (quick or
old fashioned, uncooked)
1 (12-ounce) package (2 cups)
semisweet chocolate
morsels
1 cup coarsely chopped nuts
(optional)

CHOC-OAT-CHIP COOKIES

Makes about 5 dozen

Preheat oven to 375°F. Beat together margarine and sugars until creamy. Add eggs, milk and vanilla; beat well. Add combined flour, baking soda and salt; mix well. Stir in oats, chocolate morsels and nuts; mix well. Drop by rounded tablespoonfuls onto ungreased cookie sheet.* Bake at 375°F for 9 to 10 minutes for a chewy cookie or 12 to 13 minutes for a crisp cookie. Cool 1 minute on cookie sheet; remove to wire rack. Cool completely. Store in tightly covered container.

__For Bar Cookies:__ Press dough into bottom of ungreased 13×9-inch baking pan. Bake 30 to 35 minutes or until light golden brown. Cool completely; cut into bars. Store tightly covered.   *Makes about 3 dozen*

__HIGH ALTITUDE ADJUSTMENT:__ Increase flour to 2 cups

__Variations:__ Prepare cookies as recipe directs, except substitute 1 cup of any of the following for 1 cup chocolate morsels:

Raisins	*Crushed toffee pieces*
Chopped dried apricots	*Candy coated chocolate pieces*
Dried cherries	*White chocolate baking pieces*

Choc-Oat-Chip Cookies

1 square BAKER'S®
   Unsweetened Chocolate
1⅓ cups BAKER'S® ANGEL
   FLAKE® Coconut
⅓ cup sweetened condensed
   milk
½ teaspoon vanilla

QUICK CHOCOLATE MACAROONS

Makes about 2 dozen cookies

HEAT oven to 350°F.

MELT chocolate in large microwavable bowl on HIGH 1 to 2 minutes or until almost melted, stirring after each minute. **Stir until chocolate is completely melted.** Stir in coconut, condensed milk and vanilla. Drop by teaspoonfuls, 1 inch apart, onto well-greased cookie sheets.

BAKE for 10 to 12 minutes or until set. Immediately remove from cookie sheets to cool on wire racks.

PREP TIME: 10 MINUTES
BAKE TIME: 10 TO 12 MINUTES

2½ tablespoons instant coffee
1½ tablespoons skim milk
⅓ cup light brown sugar
¼ cup granulated sugar
¼ cup margarine
1 egg
½ teaspoon almond extract
2 cups all-purpose flour, sifted
¼ cup wheat flakes cereal
½ teaspoon ground cinnamon
¼ teaspoon baking powder

MOCHA COOKIES

Makes 40 cookies

Preheat oven to 350°F. Spray cookie sheets with non-stick cooking spray. In small cup, dissolve coffee in milk. In large bowl, cream together sugars and margarine. Beat in egg, almond extract and coffee mixture. Stir together flour, wheat flakes, cinnamon and baking powder; beat into sugar mixture gradually. Drop by teaspoonfuls, 2 inches apart, onto cookie sheets. Flatten with back of fork. Bake 8 to 10 minutes or until set. Remove from cookie sheets. Cool completely.

FAVORITE RECIPE FROM THE SUGAR ASSOCIATION, INC.

COOKIES

- ½ cup butter or margarine
- 2 squares (1 ounce each) unsweetened chocolate
- 1 egg
- 1 cup packed brown sugar
- 1 teaspoon vanilla
- ½ teaspoon baking soda
- 1½ cups all-purpose flour
- ½ cup milk
- 1 package (16 ounces) large marshmallows, halved crosswise

FROSTING

- 1½ squares (1½ ounces) unsweetened chocolate
- ¼ cup butter or margarine
- 1½ cups powdered sugar
- 1 egg white*
- 1 teaspoon vanilla

Use clean, uncracked egg.

CHOCOLATE-FROSTED MARSHMALLOW COOKIES

Makes about 5 dozen cookies

To prepare Cookies: Preheat oven to 350°F. Lightly grease cookie sheets or line with parchment paper. Melt butter and chocolate in small heavy saucepan over low heat; stir to blend. Remove from heat; cool. Beat egg, brown sugar, vanilla and baking soda in large bowl until light and fluffy. Blend in chocolate mixture and flour until smooth. Slowly beat in milk to make a light, cake-batter-like dough. Drop dough by teaspoonfuls 2 inches apart onto prepared cookie sheets. Bake 10 to 12 minutes or until firm in center. Immediately place a halved marshmallow, cut side down, onto each baked cookie. Return to oven 1 minute or just until marshmallow is warm enough to stick to cookie. Remove to wire racks to cool.

To prepare Frosting: Melt chocolate and butter in small heavy saucepan over low heat; stir to blend. Beat in powdered sugar. Beat in egg white and vanilla, adding a little water, if necessary, to make a smooth, slightly soft frosting. Spoon frosting over cookies to cover marshmallows.

2 cups all-purpose flour
½ cup unsweetened cocoa
2 teaspoons baking soda
¼ teaspoon salt
⅔ cup butter or margarine,
    softened
    Sugar
¼ cup light corn syrup
1 large egg
1 teaspoon vanilla
24 large marshmallows

MARSHMALLOW SANDWICH COOKIES

Makes about 2 dozen sandwich cookies

1. Preheat oven to 350°F. Place flour, cocoa, baking soda and salt in medium bowl; stir to combine.

2. Beat butter and 1¼ cups sugar in large bowl with electric mixer at medium speed until light and fluffy. Beat in corn syrup, egg and vanilla. Gradually add flour mixture. Beat at low speed, scraping down side of bowl occasionally. Cover and refrigerate dough 15 minutes or until firm enough to roll into balls.

3. Place sugar in shallow dish. Roll tablespoonfuls of dough into 1-inch balls; roll in sugar to coat. Place 3 inches apart on ungreased cookie sheets. Bake 10 to 11 minutes or until set. Remove cookies with spatula to wire rack; cool completely.

4. To assemble sandwiches,* place 1 marshmallow on flat side of 1 cookie on paper plate. Microwave at HIGH 12 seconds or until marshmallow is hot. Immediately place another cookie, flat side down, over marshmallow; press together slightly.

5. Store tightly covered at room temperature. These cookies do not freeze well.

Cookies also taste great just as they are!

Marshmallow Sandwich Cookies

1 cup butter, softened
⅔ cup granulated sugar
1 cup packed light brown sugar
2 eggs
1 teaspoon baking soda
1 teaspoon vanilla
  Pinch salt
1 cup whole wheat flour
1 cup all-purpose flour
2 cups uncooked rolled oats
1 package (12 ounces)
    semisweet chocolate chips
1 cup sunflower seeds

WHOLE GRAIN CHIPPERS

Makes about 6 dozen cookies

Preheat oven to 375°F. Lightly grease cookie sheets or line with parchment paper. Beat butter with granulated sugar, brown sugar and eggs in large bowl until light and fluffy. Beat in baking soda, vanilla and salt. Blend in whole wheat flour, all-purpose flour and oats to make a stiff dough. Stir in chocolate chips. Shape rounded teaspoonfuls of dough into balls; roll in sunflower seeds. Place 2 inches apart on prepared cookie sheets. Bake 8 to 10 minutes or until firm. Do not overbake. Cool a few minutes on cookie sheet, then remove to wire racks to cool completely.

1 package DUNCAN HINES®
    Moist Deluxe Yellow Cake
    Mix
½ cup butter or margarine,
    melted
1 egg
1 cup semisweet chocolate chips
½ cup finely chopped pecans
1 cup sliced almonds, divided

DOUBLE NUT CHOCOLATE CHIP COOKIES

Makes 3 to 3½ dozen cookies

1. Preheat oven to 375°F. Grease cookie sheets.

2. Combine cake mix, butter and egg in large bowl. Mix at low speed with electric mixer until just blended. Stir in chocolate chips, pecans and ¼ cup almonds. Shape rounded tablespoonfuls of dough into balls. Place remaining ¾ cup almonds in shallow bowl. Press tops of cookies in almonds. Place 1 inch apart on prepared cookie sheets.

3. Bake 9 to 11 minutes or until lightly browned. Cool 2 minutes on cookie sheets. Remove to cooling racks.

Whole Grain Chippers

Pastry for single crust pie
(refrigerated or homemade)
¾ cup all-purpose flour
¼ teaspoon baking soda
¼ teaspoon salt
¾ cup granulated sugar
⅓ cup butter or margarine
2 tablespoons water
2 cups (12-ounce package)
NESTLÉ® TOLL HOUSE®
Semi-Sweet Chocolate
Morsels, divided
2 eggs
1 teaspoon vanilla extract
½ cup chopped nuts (optional)
Toppings: Nuts, toasted
coconut, sliced fruit,
berries, candy pieces, ice
cream scoops

CHOCOLATE PIZZA

Makes 12 servings

ROLL pastry to 12-inch circle; press into bottom and up sides of 10½-inch tart pan with removable bottom. Press foil onto bottom and up sides of pastry surface.

BAKE in preheated 425°F oven for 15 minutes. Remove from oven; remove foil. Reduce oven temperature to 350°F.

COMBINE flour, baking soda and salt in small bowl. Heat sugar, butter and water in medium saucepan just to boiling; remove from heat. Add *1 cup* morsels; stir until smooth. Add eggs one at a time, stirring well after each addition. Stir in flour mixture and vanilla. Stir in *remaining* morsels and nuts; pour chocolate filling into pie crust.

BAKE for 30 to 35 minutes. Cool completely in pan. Remove rim of pan. Arrange toppings over pizza; cut into wedges to serve.

2 squares (1 ounce each) unsweetened chocolate

½ cup butter or margarine, softened

1 cup packed light brown sugar

1 egg

1¼ cups all-purpose flour

¼ teaspoon baking powder

⅛ teaspoon baking soda

Dash salt

½ cup chopped walnuts or pecans

½ cup flaked coconut

Pecan halves or halved red candied cherries

CHOCOLATE-COCONUT COOKIES

Makes 4 dozen cookies

Preheat oven to 350°F. Lightly grease cookie sheets or line with parchment paper. Melt chocolate in top of double boiler over hot, not boiling, water. Remove from heat; cool. Cream butter and sugar in large bowl until blended. Add egg and melted chocolate; beat until light. Combine flour, baking powder, baking soda and salt in small bowl. Stir into creamed mixture until blended. Mix in nuts and coconut. Drop dough by teaspoonfuls 2 inches apart onto prepared cookie sheets. Press a pecan or cherry half into center of each cookie. Bake 10 to 12 minutes or until firm. Remove to wire racks to cool.

TIP: For a festive touch, top these easy-to-make cookies with red candied cherries and add them to your holiday cookie tray.

C H O C O L A T E   T I P

Unsweetened chocolate is often called bitter chocolate or baking chocolate. It is the purest form of chocolate with no added flavors or sugar. It is *used for baking because of the bitter taste. It is available in packages of individually wrapped 1-ounce squares.*

COOKIES

1 cup semi-sweet chocolate
   chips
2 squares (1 ounce each)
   unsweetened baking
   chocolate
1 cup sugar
½ BUTTER FLAVOR* CRISCO®
   Stick or ½ cup BUTTER
   FLAVOR CRISCO all-
   vegetable shortening
2 eggs
1 teaspoon salt
1 teaspoon vanilla
1½ cups plus 2 tablespoons
   all-purpose flour
½ teaspoon baking soda
¾ cup finely chopped peanuts
36 miniature peanut butter cups,
   unwrapped

DRIZZLE

1 cup peanut butter chips

*Butter Flavor Crisco is artificially
flavored*

CHOCOLATE PEANUT BUTTER CUP COOKIES

Makes about 3 dozen cookies

1. Heat oven to 350°F.

2. **For Cookies,** combine chocolate chips and chocolate squares in microwave-safe measuring cup or bowl. Microwave at MEDIUM (50% power) 2 minutes; stir. Repeat until smooth (or melt on rangetop in small saucepan on very low heat). Cool slightly.

3. Combine sugar and shortening in large bowl. Beat at medium speed of electric mixer until blended and crumbly. Beat in eggs, one at a time, then salt and vanilla. Reduce speed to low. Add chocolate slowly. Mix until well blended. Stir in flour and baking soda with spoon until well blended. Shape dough into 1¼-inch balls. Roll in nuts. Place, 2 inches apart, on ungreased cookie sheet.

4. Bake at 350°F for 8 to 10 minutes or until set. Immediately press peanut butter cup into center of each cookie. Press sides of cookie up against cup. Cool 2 minutes on cookie sheet before removing to cooling rack. Cool completely.

5. **For Drizzle,** place peanut butter chips in heavy resealable sandwich bag. Seal. Microwave at MEDIUM (50% power) 1 minute. Knead bag. Repeat until smooth (or melt by placing bag in hot water). Cut tiny tip off bottom corner of bag. Squeeze out and drizzle over cookies.

Chocolate Peanut Butter Cup Cookies

2 squares (1 ounce each) semisweet baking chocolate, coarsely chopped
1¼ cups all-purpose flour
½ teaspoon baking powder
¼ teaspoon salt
½ cup butter or margarine, softened
½ cup sugar
1 large egg
1 teaspoon vanilla
Fillings as desired:
    maraschino cherries (well drained) or candied cherries; chocolate mint candies, broken in half; white baking bar, cut into chunks; thick milk chocolate candy bar, cut into chunks or semi-sweet chocolate chunks; raspberry jam or apricot preserves
Nonpareils, for garnish

SURPRISE COOKIES

Makes 1 dozen cookies

1. Preheat oven to 350°F. Grease mini-muffin cups; set aside.

2. Melt chocolate in small, heavy saucepan over low heat, stirring constantly; set aside.

3. Place flour, baking powder and salt in small bowl; stir to combine.

4. Beat butter and sugar in large bowl with electric mixer at medium speed until light and fluffy. Beat in egg and vanilla. Gradually beat in chocolate. Gradually add flour mixture. Beat at low speed until blended.

5. Drop level teaspoonfuls of dough into prepared muffin cups. Smooth down dough and form small indentation with back of teaspoon.

6. Fill as desired with assorted filling ingredients. Top with heaping teaspoonful of dough, smoothing top lightly with back of spoon. Sprinkle tops with nonpareils, if desired.

7. Bake 15 to 17 minutes or until centers of cookies are set. Remove pan to wire rack; cool completely before removing cookies from pan.

8. Store tightly covered at room temperature. These cookies do not freeze well.

Surprise Cookies

2 cups uncooked rolled oats
¾ cup packed brown sugar
½ cup vegetable oil
½ cup finely chopped walnuts
1 egg
2 teaspoons grated orange peel
¼ teaspoon salt
1 package (12 ounces) milk
    chocolate chips

CHOCOLATE-DIPPED OAT COOKIES

Makes about 6 dozen cookies

Combine oats, sugar, oil, walnuts, egg, orange peel and salt in large bowl until blended. Cover; refrigerate overnight. Preheat oven to 350°F. Lightly grease cookie sheets or line with parchment paper. Melt chocolate chips in top of double boiler over hot, not boiling, water; set aside. Shape oat mixture into large-marble-sized balls. Place 2 inches apart on prepared cookie sheets. Bake 10 to 12 minutes or until golden and crisp. Cool 10 minutes on wire racks. Dip tops of cookies, one at a time, into melted chocolate. Place on waxed paper; cool until chocolate is set.

1 cup semi-sweet chocolate
    chips
7 tablespoons margarine or
    butter
4 cups RICE CHEX® Brand
    Cereal, crushed to 2½ cups
4 SNICKERS® candy bars
    (2.07 ounces each), cut into
    ½-inch pieces
½ cup raisins
    Powdered sugar

KARA'S KRUNCHIE KOOKIES

Makes 24 kookies

Paper line twenty-four 2½-inch muffin cups. Combine chocolate chips and margarine in saucepan. Cook over low heat until melted, stirring frequently. Stir in cereal, candy bars and raisins. Divide evenly among prepared muffins cups; press firmly onto bottom of muffin cups with back of buttered spoon or buttered hands. Chill 1 hour. Sprinkle with powdered sugar. Store in airtight container in refrigerator.

¾ **cup butter or margarine,**
   softened
⅔ **cup sugar**
3 **egg yolks**
1 **teaspoon vanilla**
¼ **teaspoon baking powder**
⅛ **teaspoon salt**
2 **cups all-purpose flour**
12 **maraschino cherries, well**
   drained and chopped
¼ **cup chopped walnuts**
¼ **cup mint-flavored or plain**
   semisweet chocolate chips
2 **teaspoons water, divided**

SPUMONI BARS

Makes 4 dozen cookies

Preheat oven to 350°F. Beat butter and sugar in large bowl until blended. Beat in egg yolks, vanilla, baking powder and salt until light in color. Stir in flour to make a stiff dough. Divide dough into 3 equal parts; place each part in small bowl. Add cherries and walnuts to one part, blending well. Melt chocolate chips in small bowl over hot water. Stir until smooth. Add melted chocolate and 1 teaspoon of the water to second part, blending well. Stir remaining 1 teaspoon water into third part. (If doughs are soft, refrigerate 10 minutes.)

Divide each color dough into 4 equal parts. Shape each part into a 6-inch rope by rolling on lightly floured surface. Place one rope of each color side by side on ungreased cookie sheet. Flatten ropes so they attach together making 1 strip of 3 colors. With rolling pin, roll strip directly on cookie sheet until it measures 12×3 inches. With straight edge of knife, score strip crosswise at 1-inch intervals. Repeat with remaining ropes to make a total of 4 tri-colored strips of dough. Bake 12 to 13 minutes or until set but not completely browned; remove from oven. While cookies are still warm, trim lengthwise edges to make them even and cut into individual cookies along score marks. (Cookies will bake together but are easy to cut apart while still warm.) Cool on cookie sheets.

½ cup firmly packed brown
  sugar
½ cup corn syrup
¼ cup (½ stick) margarine or
  butter
4 squares BAKER'S® Semi-Sweet
  Chocolate
1 cup all-purpose flour
1 cup finely chopped nuts
  Whipped cream or COOL
  WHIP® Whipped Topping,
  thawed

CHOCOLATE LACE CORNUCOPIAS

Makes about 30 cornucopias

HEAT oven to 350°F.

MICROWAVE sugar, corn syrup and margarine in large microwavable bowl on HIGH 2 minutes or until boiling. Stir in chocolate until completely melted. Gradually stir in flour and nuts until well blended.

DROP by level tablespoonfuls, 4 inches apart, onto foil-covered cookie sheets.

BAKE for 10 minutes. Lift foil and cookies onto wire rack. Cool on wire rack 3 to 4 minutes or until cookies can be easily peeled off foil. Remove foil; finish cooling cookies on wire rack that has been covered with paper towels.

PLACE several cookies, lacy side down, on foil-lined cookie sheet. Heat at 350° for 2 to 3 minutes or until slightly softened. Remove from foil, one at a time, and roll lacy side out to form cones. Cool completely. Just before serving, fill with whipped cream.

PREP TIME: 20 MINUTES
BAKE TIME: 12 TO 13 MINUTES

Saucepan preparation: Mix sugar, corn syrup and margarine in 2-quart saucepan. Bring to boil over medium heat, stirring constantly. Remove from heat; stir in chocolate until melted. Continue as above.

Chocolate Lace Cornucopias

½ cup (1 stick) butter

½ cup sugar

⅓ cup dark corn syrup

½ teaspoon ground cinnamon

¼ teaspoon ground ginger

1 cup all-purpose flour

2 teaspoons brandy

1 cup (6 ounces) NESTLÉ®
TOLL HOUSE® Semi-Sweet
Chocolate Morsels

1 tablespoon shortening

⅓ cup finely chopped nuts

CHOCOLATE-DIPPED BRANDY SNAPS

Makes about 3 dozen (2½-inch) cookies

MELT butter, sugar, corn syrup, cinnamon and ginger in medium, heavy saucepan over low heat, stirring until smooth. Remove from heat; stir in flour and brandy. Drop mixture by rounded teaspoonfuls onto ungreased baking sheets about 3 inches apart, baking no more than six cookies at a time.

BAKE in preheated 300°F for 10 to 14 minutes. Let stand a few seconds. Remove from baking sheets and immediately roll around wooden spoon handle; cool completely.

MICROWAVE morsels and shortening in medium, microwave-safe bowl on HIGH (100%) power for 45 seconds; stir. Microwave an additional 10 to 20 second intervals, stirring until smooth. Dip cookies halfway in melted chocolate; shake of excess. Sprinkle with nuts; set on waxed paper-lined cookie sheets. Chill for 10 minutes or until chocolate is set. Store in airtight container in refrigerator.

Chocolate-Dipped Brandy Snaps

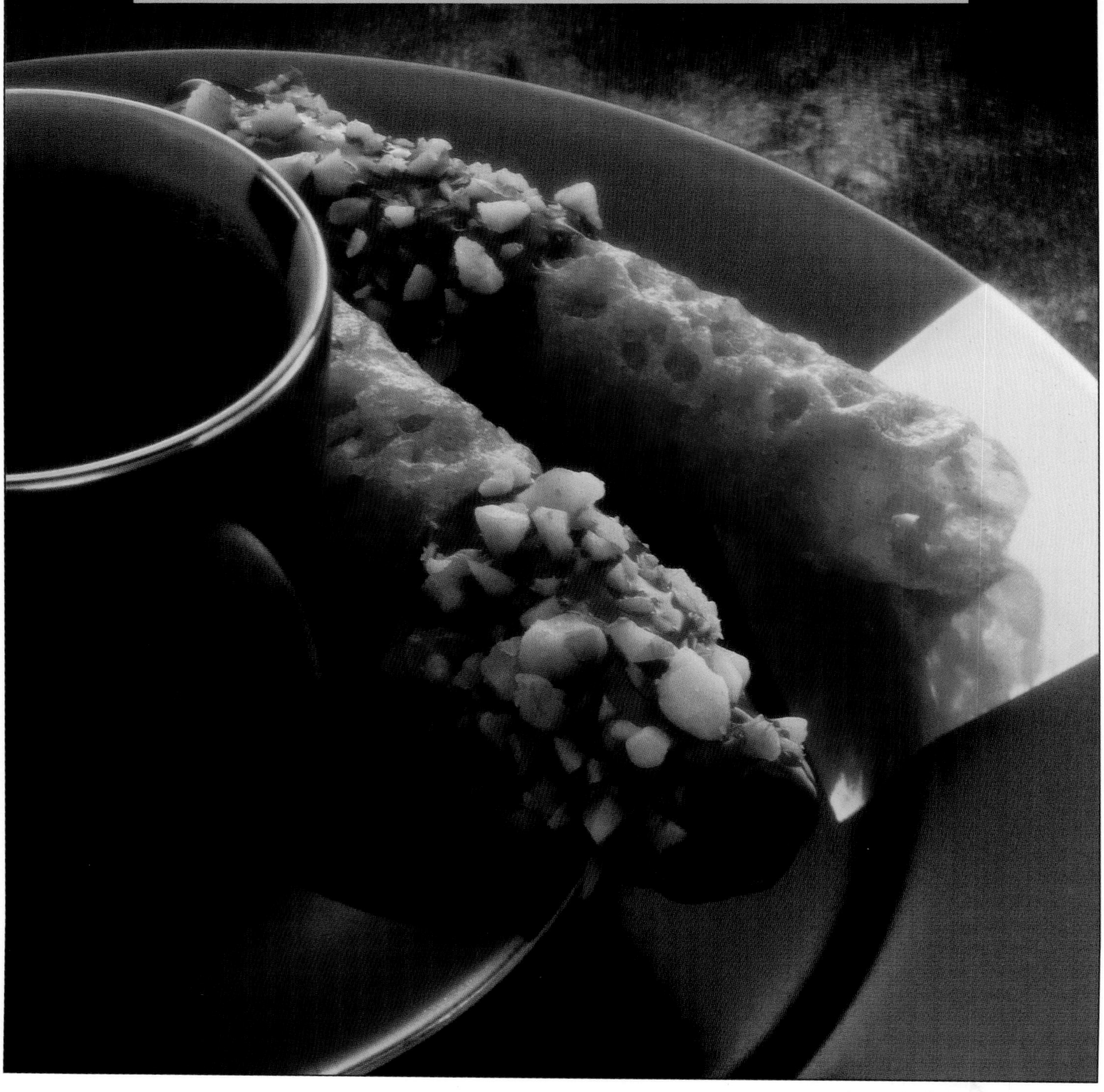

2 teaspoons butter, softened,
   divided
1¼ cups cake flour or all-purpose
   flour
¼ cup unsweetened cocoa
   powder
¼ teaspoon salt
¼ teaspoon baking powder
1 cup granulated sugar
2 large eggs
¾ cup butter, melted and cooled
2 tablespoons almond-flavored
   liqueur or kirsch
   Powdered sugar

CHOCOLATE MADELEINES

Makes about 2 dozen madeleines

1. Preheat oven to 375°F. Grease 2 madeleine pans with softened butter, 1 teaspoon per pan; dust with flour; set aside. (If only 1 madeleine pan is available, thoroughly wash, dry, regrease and flour after baking each batch. Cover remaining dough with plastic wrap; let stand at room temperature.)

2. Place flour, cocoa, salt and baking powder in medium bowl; stir to combine.

3. Beat sugar and eggs in large bowl with electric mixer at medium speed 5 minutes or until mixture is light in color, thick and falls in wide ribbons from beaters. Beat in flour mixture at low speed until well blended. Beat in melted butter and liqueur until just blended.

4. Spoon level tablespoonfuls of batter into each prepared madeleine mold. Bake 12 minutes or until puffed and golden brown.

Let madeleines stand in pan 1 minute. Carefully loosen cookies from pan with point of small knife. Invert pan over wire racks; tap lightly to release cookies. Let stand 2 minutes. Cookies should be shell-side up; cool completely.

5. Dust with sifted powdered sugar. Store tightly covered at room temperature up to 24 hours or freeze up to 3 months.

Chocolate Madeleines

2 cups (12-ounce package)
NESTLÉ® TOLL HOUSE®
Semi-Sweet Chocolate
Morsels, divided
2¾ cups all-purpose flour
1 teaspoon baking soda
½ teaspoon salt
½ teaspoon ground ginger
½ teaspoon ground cinnamon
3 tablespoons butter or
margarine, softened
3 tablespoons granulated sugar
½ cup molasses
¼ cup water
Prepared vanilla frosting or
colored icing in tubes

CHOCOLATE GINGERBREAD BOYS AND GIRLS

Makes about 2½ dozen cookies

MICROWAVE *1½ cups* morsels in medium, microwave-safe bowl on HIGH (100%) power for 1 minute; stir. Microwave an additional 10 to 20 second intervals, stirring until smooth; cool to room temperature. Combine flour, baking soda, salt, ginger and cinnamon in medium bowl.

BEAT butter and sugar in small mixer bowl until creamy; beat in molasses and melted chocolate. Gradually add flour mixture alternately with water, beating until smooth. Cover and chill 1 hour or until firm.

ROLL ½ of the dough to ¼-inch thickness on floured surface with floured rolling pin. Cut into gingerbread boy and girl shapes; place on ungreased baking sheets. Repeat with remaining dough.

BAKE in preheated 350°F oven 5 to 6 minutes or until edges are set but centers are slightly soft. Let stand for 2 minutes; remove to wire racks to cool completely.

PLACE *remaining* morsels in heavy-duty plastic bag. Microwave on HIGH (100%) power for 45 seconds; knead. Microwave for 10 seconds; knead until smooth. Cut tiny corner from bag; squeeze to pipe chocolate. Decorate with piped frosting or icing.

1 cup butter or margarine,
    softened
½ cup sugar
3 egg yolks
2 teaspoons grated orange zest
1 teaspoon orange extract
2¼ cups all-purpose flour, divided
3 tablespoons unsweetened
    cocoa
1 teaspoon vanilla
1 teaspoon chocolate extract

ORANGE & CHOCOLATE RIBBON COOKIES

Makes about 5 dozen cookies

Beat butter, sugar and egg yolks in large bowl until light and fluffy. Remove half of the mixture; place in another bowl. Add orange zest, orange extract and 1¼ cups flour to one half of the mixture; mix until blended and smooth. Shape into a ball. Add cocoa, vanilla and chocolate extract to second half of the mixture; beat until smooth. Stir in remaining 1 cup flour; mix until blended and smooth. Shape into a ball. Cover doughs; refrigerate 10 minutes.

Empty a 12×2×2-inch food wrap box, such as foil or plastic wrap; set aside. Roll out each dough separately on lightly floured surface to a 12×4-inch rectangle. Pat edges of dough to straighten; use rolling pin to level off thickness. Place one of the doughs on top of the other. Using a sharp knife, make a lengthwise cut through center of doughs. Lift half of the dough onto the other to make a long, 4-layer strip of dough. With hands, press dough strips together. Wrap in plastic wrap; fit into food wrap box, pressing down at the top. Close box; refrigerate at least 1 hour or up to 3 days. (For longer storage, freeze up to 6 weeks.)

Preheat oven to 350°F. Lightly grease cookie sheets or line with parchment paper. Cut dough crosswise into ¼-inch-thick slices; place 2 inches apart on prepared cookie sheets. Bake 10 to 12 minutes or until very lightly browned. Remove to wire racks to cool.

⅔ cup butter or margarine,
   softened

1 cup sugar

1 large egg

1 teaspoon vanilla

1¼ cups all-purpose flour

1 teaspoon baking powder

½ teaspoon salt

1 cup uncooked quick-cooking
   oats

1 cup mint chocolate chips,
   melted

MINT CHOCOLATE PINWHEELS

Makes about 3 dozen cookies

1. Beat butter and sugar in large bowl with electric mixer at medium speed. Add egg and vanilla; beat well. Gradually add flour, baking power and salt. Beat until just blended. Stir in oats with mixing spoon.

2. Divide cookie dough in half. Add melted chocolate to one half; mix well.

3. Roll out each half of dough between 2 sheets of waxed paper into 15×10-inch rectangles. Remove waxed paper from top of each rectangle.

4. Place chocolate dough over plain dough; remove bottom sheet of waxed paper from bottom of chocolate dough. Using bottom sheet of waxed paper as a guide and starting at long side, tightly roll up dough jelly-roll fashion, removing waxed paper as you roll.

5. Wrap dough in plastic wrap; refrigerate at least 2 hours or up to 24 hours.

6. Preheat oven to 350°F. Lightly grease cookie sheet.

7. Unwrap log. With long, sharp knife, cut dough into ¼-inch slices. Place 3 inches apart on prepared cookie sheets. Bake 10 to 12 minutes or until set. Remove cookies with spatula to wire racks; cool completely.

8. Store tightly covered at room temperature or freeze up to 3 months.

Mint Chocolate Pinwheels

4 ounces bittersweet chocolate
    candy bar, broken into
    pieces
3 cups all-purpose flour
½ teaspoon baking soda
½ teaspoon salt
⅔ cup butter or margarine,
    softened
¾ cup sugar
2 large eggs
2 teaspoons vanilla
   Apricot preserves

PEEK-A-BOO APRICOT COOKIES

Makes about 1½ dozen cookies

1. Melt chocolate in small bowl set in bowl of very hot water. This will take about 10 minutes.

2. Place flour, baking soda and salt in medium bowl; stir to combine.

3. Beat butter and sugar in large bowl with electric mixer at medium speed until light and fluffy. Beat in eggs, 1 at a time. Beat in vanilla and chocolate. Gradually add flour mixture. Beat at low speed until blended.

4. Divide dough into 2 rounds; flatten into discs. Wrap in plastic wrap; refrigerate 2 hours or until firm.

5. Preheat oven to 350°F. Roll out dough on lightly floured surface with stockinette-covered rolling pin to ¼- to ⅛-inch thickness. Cut out dough with 2½-inch-round cutter. Cut 1-inch centers out of half the circles. Remove scraps of dough from around and within circles; reserve. Place circles on ungreased cookie sheets. Repeat rolling and cutting with remaining scraps of dough.

6. Bake cookies 9 to 10 minutes or until set. Let cookies stand on cookie sheets 2 minutes. Remove cookies with spatula to wire rack; cool completely.

7. To assemble cookies, spread about 1½ teaspoons preserves over flat side of cookie circles; top with cut-out cookies to form a sandwich. Store tightly covered at room temperature. These cookies do not freeze well.

Peek-A-Boo Apricot Cookies

1 cup butter or margarine,
    softened
½ cup packed light brown sugar
¼ cup granulated sugar
1 egg
¼ teaspoon baking soda
2½ cups all-purpose flour
½ cup each semisweet chocolate
    chips and peanut butter
    chips, chopped*

Chips can be chopped in a food processor.

CHOCOLATE & PEANUT–BUTTER TWEED COOKIES

Makes about 6 dozen cookies

Beat butter and sugars in large bowl until smooth. Add egg and baking soda; beat until light. Stir in flour until dough is smooth. Blend in chopped chips. Divide dough into 4 parts. Shape each part into a roll, about 1½ inches in diameter. Wrap in plastic wrap; refrigerate until firm, at least 1 hour or up to 2 weeks. (For longer storage, freeze up to 6 weeks.)

Preheat oven to 375°F. Lightly grease cookie sheets or line with parchment paper. Cut rolls into ⅛-inch-thick slices; place 2 inches apart on prepared cookie sheets. Bake 10 to 12 minutes or until lightly browned. Remove to wire racks to cool.

CINNAMON–CHOCOLATE CUTOUTS

Makes about 6 dozen cookies

2 squares (1 ounce each) unsweetened chocolate

½ cup butter or margarine, softened

1 cup granulated sugar

1 egg

1 teaspoon vanilla

3 cups all-purpose flour

2 teaspoons ground cinnamon

½ teaspoon baking soda

¼ teaspoon salt

½ cup sour cream

Decorator Icing (recipe follows)

Melt chocolate in top of double boiler over hot, not boiling, water. Remove from heat; cool. Cream butter, melted chocolate, granulated sugar, egg and vanilla in large bowl until light. Combine flour, cinnamon, baking soda and salt in small bowl. Stir into creamed mixture with sour cream until smooth. Cover; refrigerate at least 30 minutes.

Preheat oven to 400°F. Lightly grease cookie sheets or line with parchment paper. Roll out dough, one fourth at a time, ¼ inch thick on lightly floured surface. Cut out with cookie cutters. Place 2 inches apart on prepared cookie sheets. Bake 10 minutes or until lightly browned, but not dark. Remove to wire racks to cool. Prepare Decorator Icing. Spoon into pastry bag fitted with small tip or small heavy-duty plastic bag. (If using plastic bag, close securely. With scissors, snip off small corner from one side of bag.) Decorate cookies with icing.

DECORATOR ICING

1 egg white*

3½ cups powdered sugar

1 teaspoon almond or lemon extract

2 to 3 tablespoons water

Use clean, uncracked egg.

Beat egg white in large bowl until frothy. Gradually beat in powdered sugar until blended. Add almond extract and enough water to moisten. Beat until smooth and glossy.

CRUST

- 1 cup uncooked rolled oats
- ½ cup all-purpose flour
- ½ cup firmly packed light brown sugar
- ¼ cup MOTT'S® Natural Apple Sauce
- 1 tablespoon margarine, melted
- ¼ teaspoon baking soda

FILLING

- ⅔ cup all-purpose flour
- ½ teaspoon baking powder
- ¼ teaspoon salt
- ¾ cup granulated sugar
- ¼ cup MOTT'S® Natural Apple Sauce
- 1 whole egg
- 1 egg white
- 2 tablespoons unsweetened cocoa powder
- 1 tablespoon margarine, melted
- ½ teaspoon vanilla extract
- ¼ cup low-fat buttermilk

ICING

- 1 cup powdered sugar
- 1 tablespoon unsweetened cocoa powder
- 1 tablespoon skim milk
- 1 teaspoon instant coffee powder

TRI-LAYER CHOCOLATE OATMEAL BARS

Makes 14 servings

1. Preheat oven to 350°F. Spray 8-inch square baking pan with nonstick cooking spray.

2. **To prepare Crust,** in medium bowl, combine oats, ½ cup flour, brown sugar, ¼ cup apple sauce, 1 tablespoon margarine and baking soda. Stir with fork until mixture resembles coarse crumbs. Press evenly into bottom of prepared pan. Bake 10 minutes.

3. **To prepare Filling,** in small bowl, combine ⅔ cup flour, baking powder and salt.

4. In large bowl, combine granulated sugar, ¼ cup apple sauce, whole egg, egg white, 2 tablespoons cocoa, 1 tablespoon margarine and vanilla.

5. Add flour mixture to apple sauce mixture alternately with buttermilk; stir until well blended. Spread filling over baked crust.

6. Bake 25 minutes or until toothpick inserted in center comes out clean. Cool completely on wire rack.

7. **To prepare Icing,** in small bowl, combine powdered sugar, 1 tablespoon cocoa, milk and coffee powder until smooth. Spread evenly over bars. Let stand until set. Run tip of knife through icing to score. Cut into 14 bars.

Tri-Layer Chocolate Oatmeal Bars

CHOCOLATE SCOTCHEROOS

Makes about 24 bars

1 cup light corn syrup
1 cup sugar
1 cup peanut butter
6 cups KELLOGGS'® RICE KRISPIES® Cereal
1 package (6 ounces, 1 cup) semi-sweet chocolate morsels
1 package (6 ounces, 1 cup) butterscotch morsels
Vegetable cooking spray

1. Measure corn syrup and sugar into large saucepan. Cook over medium heat, stirring frequently, until sugar dissolves and mixture begins to boil. Remove from heat. Stir in peanut butter; mix well. Add Kellogg's® Rice Krispies® Cereal. Stir until well coated. Press mixture into 13×9×2-inch pan coated with cooking spray. Set aside.

2. Melt chocolate and butterscotch morsels together in small saucepan over low heat, stirring constantly. Spread evenly over cereal mixture. Let stand until firm. Cut into bars when cool.

OREO® DECADENCE BARS

Makes 16 bars

1 (8-ounce) package OREO® Crunchies
2 tablespoons FLEISCHMANN'S® Margarine, melted
¾ cup white chocolate chips
¾ cup miniature marshmallows
¾ cup PLANTERS® Walnuts, chopped
1 (14-ounce) can sweetened condensed milk

Preheat oven to 350°F. In small bowl, combine Crunchies and margarine. Sprinkle 1 cup crumb mixture over bottom of lightly greased 8×8×2-inch baking pan. Sprinkle with white chocolate chips, marshmallows and walnuts; top with remaining crumbs. Pour condensed milk evenly over crumbs. Bake at 350°F for 30 minutes. Cool completely in pan. Cut into bars; store in airtight container.

Chocolate Scotcheroos

CRISPY CHOCOLATE BARS

Makes 32 bars

1 package (6 ounces, 1 cup) semi-sweet chocolate chips
1 package (6 ounces, 1 cup) butterscotch chips
½ cup peanut butter
5 cups KELLOGG'S CORN FLAKES® cereal
Vegetable cooking spray

1. In large saucepan, combine chocolate and butterscotch chips and peanut butter. Stir over low heat until smooth. Remove from heat.

2. Add Kellogg's Corn Flakes® cereal. Stir until well coated.

3. Using buttered spatula or waxed paper, press mixture evenly into 9×9×2-inch pan coated with cooking spray. Cut into bars when cool.

APPLESAUCE FUDGE BARS

Makes about 3 dozen bars

3 squares (1 ounce each) semisweet chocolate
½ cup butter or margarine
⅔ cup unsweetened applesauce
2 eggs, beaten
1 cup packed light brown sugar
1 teaspoon vanilla
1 cup all-purpose flour
½ teaspoon baking powder
¼ teaspoon baking soda
½ cup walnuts, chopped
1 cup (6 ounces) milk chocolate chips

Preheat oven to 350°F. Grease a 9-inch square pan. Melt semisweet chocolate and butter in small heavy saucepan over low heat. Remove from heat; cool. Combine applesauce, eggs, sugar and vanilla in large bowl. Combine flour, baking powder and baking soda in small bowl. Mix dry ingredients into applesauce mixture; blend in chocolate mixture. Spread batter evenly in prepared pan. Sprinkle nuts over the top. Bake 25 to 30 minutes or just until set. Remove from oven; sprinkle chocolate chips over the top. Let stand a few minutes until chips melt; spread evenly over bars. Cool in pan on wire rack. Cut into 2×1-inch bars.

1 package DUNCAN HINES®
    Moist Deluxe Devil's Food
    Cake Mix

FILLING
    ½ cup butter or margarine,
        softened
    ½ CRISCO® Stick or ½ cup
        CRISCO all-vegetable
        shortening
    1 cup granulated sugar
    2 cans (5 ounces each)
        evaporated milk (1¼ cups)
    1 tablespoon vanilla extract

GLAZE
    2 cups sifted confectioners'
        sugar
    2 packets (1 ounce each)
        unsweetened pre-melted
        chocolate
    ¼ cup hot melted butter
    4 tablespoons boiling water,
        divided

CHOCOLATE CREAM–FILLED SQUARES

Makes 24 Servings

1. Preheat oven to 350°F. Grease and flour 15½×10½×1-inch jelly-roll pan.

2. Prepare cake following package directions for original recipe. Pour batter into pan. Bake at 350°F for 20 to 24 minutes or until toothpick inserted in center comes out clean. Cool completely.

3. **For filling,** place ½ cup butter in large bowl. Beat at medium speed with electric mixer for 5 minutes. Add shortening gradually, beating for 4 minutes. Add granulated sugar gradually, beating until well blended. Add evaporated milk and vanilla extract. (It is normal for mixture to separate.) Beat for 8 minutes or until smooth and creamy. Spread over cake. Refrigerate.

4. **For glaze,** combine confectioners' sugar, pre-melted chocolate, melted butter and 3 tablespoons boiling water in small bowl. Stir until blended. Add remaining 1 tablespoon water. Beat until smooth. Spread immediately over filling. Refrigerate until ready to serve.

TIP: You may also bake this cake in a greased and floured 13×9×2-inch pan at 350°F for 35 to 38 minutes or until toothpick inserted in center comes out clean.

2 cups butter, softened, divided
½ cup granulated sugar, divided
1 large egg
2¾ cups all-purpose flour
⅔ cup packed light brown sugar
¼ cup light corn syrup
2½ cups coarsely chopped pecans
1 cup semisweet chocolate chips

CHOCOLATE CARAMEL PECAN BARS

Makes 30 bars

1. Preheat oven to 375°F. Grease 15×10-inch jelly-roll pan; set aside.

2. Beat 1 cup butter and granulated sugar in large bowl with electric mixer at medium speed until light and fluffy. Beat in egg. Add flour. Beat at low speed until just blended. Spread dough into prepared pan. Bake 20 minutes or until light golden brown.

3. While bars are baking, prepare topping. Combine remaining 1 cup butter, brown sugar and corn syrup in medium, heavy saucepan. Cook over medium heat until mixture boils, stirring frequently. Boil gently 2 minutes, without stirring. Quickly stir in pecans and spread topping evenly over base. Return to oven and bake 20 minutes or until dark golden brown and bubbling.

4. Immediately sprinkle chocolate chips evenly over hot caramel. Gently press chips into caramel topping with spatula. Loosen caramel from edges of pan with a thin spatula or knife. Remove pan to wire rack; cool completely. Cut into 3×1½-inch bars.

5. Store tightly covered at room temperature or freeze up to 3 months.

Chocolate Caramel Pecan Bars

¼ cup (½ stick) **margarine or**
  butter
1½ cups **graham cracker crumbs**
¾ cup **sugar**
1 package (4 ounces) **BAKER'S®**
  GERMAN'S® Sweet
  Chocolate
1 package (8 ounces)
  PHILADELPHIA BRAND®
  Cream Cheese, softened
1 **egg**
1 cup **BAKER'S® ANGEL**
  FLAKE® Coconut
1 cup **chopped nuts**

LAYERED CHOCOLATE CHEESE BARS

Makes about 24 bars

HEAT oven to 350°F.

MELT margarine in oven in 13×9-inch pan. Add graham cracker crumbs and ¼ cup of the sugar; mix well. Press into pan. Bake for 10 minutes.

MELT chocolate. Stir in remaining ½ cup sugar, cream cheese and egg. Spread over crust. Sprinkle with coconut and nuts; press lightly.

BAKE for 30 minutes. Cool; cut into bars.

PREP TIME: 20 MINUTES
BAKE TIME: 40 MINUTES

*Top plate (clockwise from top): Layered Chocolate
Cheese Bars, Banana Split Bars (page 99) and
Chocolate Peanut Butter Bars (page 98)*

2 cups peanut butter

1 cup sugar

2 eggs

1 package (8 ounces) BAKER'S®
  Semi-Sweet Chocolate

1 cup chopped peanuts

CHOCOLATE PEANUT BUTTER BARS

Makes about 24 bars

HEAT oven to 350°F.

BEAT peanut butter, sugar and eggs in large bowl until light and fluffy. Reserve 1 cup peanut butter mixture; set aside.

MELT 4 squares chocolate. Add to peanut butter mixture in bowl; mix well. Press into ungreased 13×9-inch pan. Top with reserved peanut butter mixture.

BAKE for 30 minutes or until edges are lightly browned. Melt remaining 4 squares chocolate; spread evenly over entire surface. Sprinkle with peanuts. Cool in pan until chocolate is set. Cut into bars.

PREP TIME: 15 MINUTES

BAKE TIME: 30 MINUTES

CHOCOLATE TIP

Chocolate should be melted gently to prevent scorching. Using the microwave is a quick and easy way to melt chocolate. Place chocolate in a small microwavable container and microwave at HIGH about 60 seconds per ounce of chocolate. The chocolate will retain its shape even when almost melted, so it is important to stir it several times during the process.

⅓ cup margarine or butter,
    softened
1 cup sugar
1 egg
1 banana, mashed
½ teaspoon vanilla
1¼ cups all-purpose flour
1 teaspoon CALUMET® Baking
    Powder
¼ teaspoon salt
⅓ cup chopped nuts
2 cups KRAFT® Miniature
    Marshmallows
1 cup BAKER'S® Semi-Sweet
    Real Chocolate Chips
⅓ cup maraschino cherries,
    drained and quartered

BANANA SPLIT BARS

Makes about 24 bars

PREHEAT oven to 350°F. Beat margarine and sugar until light and fluffy. Add egg, banana and vanilla; mix well. Mix in flour, baking powder and salt. Stir in nuts. Pour batter into greased 13×9-inch pan.

BAKE for 20 minutes. Remove from oven. Sprinkle with marshmallows, chips and cherries. Bake 10 to 15 minutes longer or until wooden toothpick inserted in center comes out clean. Cool in pan; cut into bars.

24 graham cracker squares
1 cup semisweet chocolate chips
1 cup flaked coconut
¾ cup coarsely chopped walnuts
1 can (14 ounces) sweetened
   condensed milk

NO-FUSS BAR COOKIES

Makes 20 bars

1. Preheat oven to 350°F. Grease 13×9-inch baking pan; set aside.

2. Place graham crackers in food processor. Process until crackers form fine crumbs. Measure 2 cups of crumbs.

3. Combine crumbs, chips, coconut and walnuts in medium bowl; stir to blend. Add milk; stir with mixing spoon until blended.

4. Spread batter evenly into prepared pan. Bake 15 to 18 minutes or until edges are golden brown. Let pan stand on wire rack until completely cooled. Cut into 2¼×2¼-inch bars.

5. Store tightly covered at room temperature or freeze up to 3 months.

No-Fuss Bar Cookies

Bar Cookie Crust (page 104)
½ cup packed brown sugar
⅓ cup KARO® Light Corn Syrup
¼ cup MAZOLA® Margarine
¼ cup heavy or whipping cream
1½ cups cocktail or dry roasted
   peanuts
1 teaspoon vanilla
⅓ cup (2 ounces) semisweet
   chocolate chips

CHOCOLATE–TOPPED PEANUT BARS

Makes about 32 bars

1. Preheat oven to 350°F. Prepare Bar Cookie Crust according to recipe directions.

2. Meanwhile, for filling, in heavy 2-quart saucepan combine brown sugar, corn syrup, margarine and cream. Bring to boil over medium heat; remove from heat. Stir in peanuts and vanilla. Pour over hot crust; spread evenly.

3. Bake 12 to 15 minutes or until filling is set around edges and center is slightly firm. Remove pan to wire rack.

4. Sprinkle with chocolate; let stand 5 minutes. Spread chocolate randomly with tip of knife. Cool. Refrigerate 15 minutes to set chocolate. Cut into 2×1½-inch bars.

From left to right: Chocolate-Topped Peanut Bars and Chocolate Pecan Pie Bars (page 104)

Bar Cookie Crust (recipe
   follows)
¾ cup KARO® Light or Dark
   Corn Syrup
3 squares (1 ounce each)
   semisweet chocolate or
   ½ cup (3 ounces) semisweet
   chocolate chips
½ cup sugar
2 eggs, slightly beaten
1 teaspoon vanilla
1¼ cups coarsely chopped pecans

CHOCOLATE PECAN PIE BARS

Makes about 32 bars

1. Preheat oven to 350°F. Prepare Bar Cookie Crust according to recipe directions.

2. Meanwhile, for filling, in heavy 3-quart saucepan stir corn syrup and chocolate over low heat just until chocolate melts. Remove from heat. Stir in sugar, eggs and vanilla until blended. Stir in pecans. Pour over hot crust; spread evenly. Bake 20 minutes or until filling is firm around edges and slightly soft in center. Cool completely on wire rack. Cut into 2×1½-inch bars.

BAR COOKIE CRUST

MAZOLA NO STICK® Corn Oil Cooking Spray
2 cups flour
½ cup (1 stick) cold MAZOLA® Margarine or butter,
   cut into pieces
⅓ cup sugar
¼ teaspoon salt

1. Preheat oven to 350°F. Spray 13×9×2-inch baking pan with cooking spray.

2. In large bowl with mixer at medium speed, beat remaining ingredients until mixture resembles coarse crumbs. Press firmly into bottom and ¼ inch up sides of prepared pan. Bake 15 minutes or until golden brown. Top with desired filling. Complete as recipe directs.

PREP TIME: 10 MINUTES
BAKE TIME: 15 MINUTES

¾ **BUTTER FLAVOR* CRISCO®
Stick or ¾ cup BUTTER
FLAVOR CRISCO
all-vegetable shortening**
2 **eggs**
½ **cup granulated sugar**
¼ **cup firmly packed brown
sugar**
1½ **teaspoons vanilla**
1 **teaspoon almond extract**
2 **cups all-purpose flour**
1 **teaspoon baking soda**
½ **teaspoon cinnamon**
1 **can (21 ounces) cherry pie
filling**
1½ **cups milk chocolate chips
Powdered sugar**

**Butter Flavor Crisco is artificially
flavored.*

"CORDIALLY YOURS" CHOCOLATE CHIP BARS

Makes 30 bars

1. Preheat oven to 350°F. Grease 15½×10½×1-inch pan with shortening.

2. Combine shortening, eggs, granulated sugar, brown sugar, vanilla and almond extract in large bowl. Beat at medium speed of electric mixer until well blended.

3. Combine flour, baking soda and cinnamon. Mix into creamed mixture at low speed until just blended. Stir in pie filling and chocolate chips. Spread in pan.

4. Bake 25 minutes or until lightly browned and top springs back when lightly pressed. Cool completely in pan on wire rack. Sprinkle with powdered sugar. Cut into 2½×2-inch bars.

½ cup uncooked rolled oats

1½ cups all-purpose flour

2 teaspoons baking powder

½ teaspoon baking soda

½ teaspoon salt

1 cup sugar

½ cup MOTT'S® Natural Apple Sauce

1 whole egg

1 egg white

2 tablespoons vegetable oil

⅓ cup low-fat buttermilk

2 tablespoons unsweetened cocoa powder

1 large ripe banana, mashed (⅔ cup)

BANANA COCOA MARBLED BARS

Makes 14 servings

1. Preheat oven to 350°F. Spray 9-inch square baking pan with nonstick cooking spray.

2. Place oats in food processor or blender; process until finely ground.

3. In medium bowl, combine oats, flour, baking powder, baking soda and salt.

4. In large bowl, combine sugar, apple sauce, whole egg, egg white and oil.

5. Add flour mixture to apple sauce mixture; stir until well blended. (Mixture will look dry.)

6. Remove 1 cup of batter to small bowl. Add buttermilk and cocoa; mix well.

7. Add banana to remaining batter. Mix well; spread into prepared pan.

8. Drop tablespoonfuls of cocoa batter over banana batter. Run knife through batters to marble.

9. Bake 35 minutes or until toothpick inserted in center comes out clean. Cool on wire rack 15 minutes; cut into 14 bars.

Banana Cocoa Marbled Bars

1 cup (6 ounces) semisweet
chocolate pieces

⅓ cup (5 tablespoons plus
1 teaspoon) margarine or
butter

16 large marshmallows

1 teaspoon vanilla

2 cups QUAKER® Oats (quick or
old fashioned, uncooked)

1 cup (any combination of)
raisins, diced dried mixed
fruit, flaked coconut,
miniature marshmallows or
chopped nuts

CHEWY CHOCOLATE NO-BAKES

Makes 3 dozen

In large saucepan over low heat, melt chocolate pieces,
margarine and marshmallows stirring until smooth.
Remove from heat; cool slightly. Stir in remaining
ingredients. Drop by rounded teaspoonfuls onto wax
paper. Chill 2 to 3 hours. Let stand at room temperature
about 15 minutes before serving. Store in tightly covered
container in refrigerator.

*Microwave Directions: Place chocolate pieces, margarine and
marshmallows in large microwavable bowl. Microwave on
HIGH 1 to 2 minutes or until mixture is melted and smooth,
stirring every 30 seconds. Proceed as recipe directs.*

Chewy Chocolate No-Bakes

½ cup butter or margarine, softened

¾ cup packed brown sugar

1 teaspoon vanilla

1 egg

½ teaspoon baking soda

¼ teaspoon salt

1 cup plus 2 tablespoons all-purpose flour

1 cup (6 ounces) semisweet chocolate chips, divided

1 cup (6 ounces) white chocolate chips, divided

½ cup chopped walnuts or pecans

MISSISSIPPI MUD BARS

Makes about 3 dozen bars

Preheat oven to 375°F. Line a 9-inch square pan with foil; grease foil. Beat butter and sugar in large bowl until blended and smooth. Beat in vanilla and egg until light. Blend in baking soda and salt. Add flour, mixing until well blended. Stir in ¾ cup semisweet chips and ¾ cup white chocolate chips and the nuts. Spread dough in prepared pan. Bake 23 to 25 minutes or until center feels firm. Do not overbake. Remove from oven; sprinkle remaining ¼ cup semisweet chips and ¼ cup white chocolate chips over the top. Let stand a few minutes until chips melt; spread evenly over bars. Cool in pan on wire rack until chocolate is set. Cut into 2×1-inch bars.

CHOCOLATE TIP

In 1502, Christopher Columbus had his first encounter with cocoa beans. Having landed in Nicaragua during his fourth voyage to America he met natives who used cocoa beans as currency as well as in the preparation of a delightful drink. But, unfortunately Columbus was too interested in his search for the sea route to India to take interest in the cocoa beans.

2 cups all-purpose flour

1 cup granulated sugar

¼ teaspoon salt

2 cups (4 sticks) butter or
  margarine, divided

1 cup packed light brown sugar

⅓ cup light corn syrup

1 cup (6 ounces) semisweet
  chocolate chips

GOOEY CARAMEL CHOCOLATE BARS

Makes 3 dozen bars

Preheat oven to 350°F. Line 13×9-inch baking pan with foil. Combine flour, granulated sugar and salt in medium bowl; stir until blended. Cut in 14 tablespoons (1¾ sticks) butter until mixture resembles coarse crumbs. Press into bottom of prepared pan.

Bake 18 to 20 minutes until lightly browned around edges. Remove pan to wire rack; cool completely.

Combine 1 cup (2 sticks) butter, brown sugar and corn syrup in heavy medium saucepan. Cook over medium heat 5 to 8 minutes until mixture boils, stirring frequently. Boil gently 2 minutes, without stirring. Immediately pour over cooled base; spread evenly to edges of pan with metal spatula. Cool completely.

Melt chocolate in double boiler over hot (not boiling) water. Stir in remaining 2 tablespoons butter. Pour over cooled caramel layer and spread evenly to edges of pan with metal spatula. Refrigerate 10 to 15 minutes until chocolate begins to set. Remove; cool completely. Cut into bars.

1 package DUNCAN HINES®
   Chocolate Chip Cookie Mix
½ cup seedless red raspberry
   jam

CHOCOLATE CHIP RASPBERRY JUMBLES

Makes 16 bars

1. Preheat oven to 350°F.

2. Prepare chocolate chip cookie mix following package directions for original recipe. Reserve ½ cup dough.

3. Spread remaining dough into ungreased 9-inch square pan. Spread jam over base. Drop reserved dough by measuring teaspoonfuls randomly over jam. Bake at 350°F for 20 to 25 minutes or until golden brown. Cool completely. Cut into bars.

1½ cups all-purpose flour
 ½ cup packed brown sugar
 ½ cup granulated sugar
1½ teaspoons baking powder
 ½ teaspoon salt
 ⅓ cup butter, softened
 2 eggs, slightly beaten
 2 cups (12 ounces) semisweet
   chocolate chips
 1 cup coarsely chopped
   California walnuts
 2 tablespoons grated orange
   peel

WALNUT–ORANGE CHOCOLATE CHIPPERS

Makes 36 squares

Combine flour, brown sugar, granulated sugar, baking powder and salt in large bowl; mix in butter and eggs. Add remaining ingredients and mix thoroughly (batter will be stiff). Spread dough evenly into greased and floured 9-inch square pan (use wet hands to smooth). Bake at 350°F 25 minutes or until golden brown. Cool; cut into squares.

FAVORITE RECIPE FROM WALNUT MARKETING BOARD

Chocolate Chip Raspberry Jumbles

⅔ cup QUAKER® Oat Bran hot
    cereal, uncooked
⅔ cup all-purpose flour
½ cup granulated sugar
⅓ cup unsweetened cocoa
½ cup mashed ripe banana
    (about 1 large)
¼ cup liquid vegetable oil
    margarine
3 tablespoons light corn syrup
2 egg whites, slightly beaten
1 teaspoon vanilla
2 teaspoons unsweetened cocoa
2 teaspoons liquid vegetable oil
    margarine
¼ cup powdered sugar
2 to 2½ teaspoons warm water,
    divided
    Strawberry halves (optional)

COCOA BANANA BARS

Heat oven to 350°F. Lightly spray 8-inch square baking pan with no-stick cooking spray or oil lightly. Combine oat bran, flour, granulated sugar and ⅓ cup cocoa. Add combined banana, ¼ cup margarine, corn syrup, egg whites and vanilla; mix well. Pour into prepared pan, spreading evenly. Bake 23 to 25 minutes or until center is set. Cool on wire rack; cut into bars. Store tightly covered.

Combine 2 teaspoons cocoa and 2 teaspoons margarine. Stir in powdered sugar and 1 teaspoon of the water. Gradually add remaining 1 to 1½ teaspoons water to make medium-thick glaze; mixing well. Drizzle glaze over brownies. Top with strawberry halves, if desired.

Cocoa Banana Bars

4 squares BAKER'S®
    Unsweetened Chocolate
¾ cup (1½ sticks) margarine or
    butter
2 cups sugar
3 eggs
1 teaspoon vanilla
1 cup all-purpose flour
1 cup chopped nuts (optional)

ONE BOWL® BROWNIES

Makes about 24 fudgy brownies

HEAT oven to 350°F. (325 °F for a glass dish). Line 13×9-inch baking pan with foil extending over edges to form handles. Grease foil.

MICROWAVE chocolate and margarine in large microwavable bowl on HIGH 2 minutes or until margarine is melted. **Stir until chocolate is completely melted.**

STIR sugar into melted chocolate mixture until well blended. Mix in eggs and vanilla. Stir in flour and nuts until well blended. Spread in prepared pan.

BAKE for 30 to 35 minutes or until toothpick inserted into center comes out with fudgy crumbs. **Do not overbake.** Cool in pan. Lift out of pan onto cutting board. Cut into squares.

PREP TIME: 10 MINUTES
BAKE TIME: 30 TO 35 MINUTES

TIPS: For cakelike brownies, stir in ½ cup milk with eggs and vanilla. Increase flour to 1½ cups.

One Bowl® Brownies

FANCY WALNUT BROWNIES

Makes 24 Brownies

BROWNIES

1 package DUNCAN HINES®
   Walnut Brownie Mix

1 egg

⅓ cup water

⅓ cup CRISCO® Oil or CRISCO®
   PURITAN® Canola Oil

GLAZE

4½ cups confectioners' sugar

½ cup milk or water

24 walnut halves, for garnish

CHOCOLATE DRIZZLE

⅓ cup semi-sweet chocolate
   chips

1 tablespoon CRISCO®
   all-vegetable shortening

1. Preheat oven to 350°F. Place 24 (2-inch) foil liners on baking sheets.

2. **For brownies,** combine brownie mix, egg, water and oil in large bowl. Stir with spoon until well blended, about 50 strokes. Stir in contents of walnut packet from Mix. Fill foil liners with 2 generous tablespoons batter. Bake at 350°F for 20 to 25 minutes or until set. Cool completely. Remove liners. Turn brownies upside down on cooling rack.

3. **For glaze,** combine confectioners' sugar and milk in medium bowl. Blend until smooth. Spoon glaze over first brownie to completely cover. Top immediately with walnut half. Repeat with remaining brownies. Allow glaze to set.

4. **For chocolate drizzle,** place chocolate chips and shortening in resealable plastic bag; seal. Place bag in bowl of hot water for several minutes. Dry with paper towel. Knead until blended and chocolate is smooth. Snip pinpoint hole in corner of bag. Drizzle chocolate over brownies. Store in single layer in airtight containers.

TIP: Place waxed paper under cooling rack to catch excess glaze.

Fancy Walnut Brownies

6 squares BAKER'S® Semi-Sweet
  Chocolate
½ cup (1 stick) margarine or
  butter
⅔ cup sugar
2 eggs
1 teaspoon vanilla
1 cup all-purpose flour
⅓ cup chopped nuts (optional)

SEMI–SWEET CHOCOLATE BROWNIES

Makes about 16 brownies

HEAT oven to 350°F.

MICROWAVE chocolate and margarine in large
microwavable bowl on HIGH 2 minutes or until margarine
is melted. **Stir until chocolate is completely melted.**

STIR sugar into melted chocolate mixture. Mix in eggs and
vanilla until well blended. Stir in flour and nuts. Spread in
greased 8-inch square pan.

BAKE for 30 minutes or until toothpick inserted into
center comes out with fudgy crumbs. **Do not overbake.**
Cool in pan; cut into squares.

PREP TIME: 10 MINUTES
BAKE TIME: 30 MINUTES

CHOCOLATE TIP

*Semisweet chocolate is pure chocolate combined
with sugar and extra cocoa butter. It is sold in a
variety of forms, including 1-ounce squares, bars,*
*chips and chunks. It is interchangeable with
bittersweet chocolate in most recipes.*

1⅓ cups unsweetened cocoa
    powder

1 cup all-purpose flour

1 teaspoon baking powder

½ teaspoon baking soda

½ teaspoon salt

⅓ cup Prune Purée (page 140) or
    prepared prune butter or
    1 jar (2½ ounces) first-stage
    baby food prunes

¼ cup nonfat milk

1 tablespoon vegetable oil

1 tablespoon instant espresso
    coffee powder or
    2 tablespoons instant coffee
    granules

1 tablespoon vanilla

6 egg whites

2 cups sugar

⅔ cup semisweet chocolate chips

FUDGY DOUBLE CHOCOLATE BROWNIES

Makes 20 brownies

Preheat oven to 325°F. Coat 15½×10½×1-inch baking pan with vegetable cooking spray. In medium bowl, combine cocoa, flour, baking powder, baking soda and salt; set aside. In small bowl, whisk together prune purée, milk, oil, espresso powder and vanilla until well blended, about 1 minute. In mixer bowl, beat egg whites and sugar on medium speed 30 seconds; increase speed to high and beat 2½ minutes more until mixture is thick, but not stiff. Add prune purée mixture; beat until well blended, about 15 seconds. Fold in flour mixture. Fold in chocolate chips. Spread batter evenly in prepared pan. Bake in center of oven 25 to 30 minutes or until springy to the touch and pick inserted into center comes out almost clean. Cool completely in pan on wire rack. Cut into bars with knife dipped into hot water.

FAVORITE RECIPE FROM CALIFORNIA PRUNE BOARD

PRALINE BROWNIES

Makes 16 brownies

BROWNIES

- **1 package DUNCAN HINES® Milk Chocolate Chunk Brownie Mix**
- **2 eggs**
- **⅓ cup water**
- **⅓ cup CRISCO® Oil or CRISCO® PURITAN® Canola Oil**
- **¾ cup chopped pecans**

TOPPING

- **¾ cup firmly packed brown sugar**
- **¾ cup chopped pecans**
- **¼ cup butter or margarine, melted**
- **2 tablespoons milk**
- **½ teaspoon vanilla extract**

1. Preheat oven to 350°F. Grease 9-inch square pan.

2. **For brownies,** combine brownie mix, eggs, water, oil and ¾ cup pecans in large bowl. Stir with spoon until well blended, about 50 strokes. Spread in pan. Bake at 350°F for 35 to 40 minutes. Remove from oven.

3. **For topping,** combine brown sugar, ¾ cup pecans, melted butter, milk and vanilla extract in small bowl. Stir with spoon until well blended. Spread over hot brownies. Return to oven. Bake for 15 minutes or until topping is set. Cool completely. Cut into bars.

Praline Brownies

1 cup all-purpose flour
¾ cup packed light brown sugar
¼ cup unsweetened cocoa
    powder
1 egg
2 egg whites
5 tablespoons margarine,
    melted
¼ cup skim milk
¼ cup honey
1 teaspoon vanilla
2 tablespoons semisweet
    chocolate chips
2 tablespoons coarsely chopped
    walnuts
Powdered sugar (optional)

BAMBOOZLERS

Makes 12 servings

1. Preheat oven to 350°F. Grease and flour 8-inch square baking pan; set aside.

2. Combine flour, brown sugar and cocoa in medium bowl. Blend together egg, egg whites, margarine, milk, honey and vanilla in medium bowl. Add to flour mixture; mix well. Pour into prepared baking pan; sprinkle with chocolate chips and walnuts.

3. Bake 30 minutes or until they spring back when lightly touched in center. Cool completely in pan on wire rack. Sprinkle with powdered sugar just before serving.

PEANUTTERS: Substitute peanut butter chips for chocolate chips and peanuts for walnuts.

BUTTERSCOTCH BABIES: Substitute butterscotch chips for chocolate chips and pecans for walnuts.

BROWNIE SUNDAES: Serve brownies on dessert plates. Top each brownie with a scoop of vanilla nonfat frozen yogurt and 2 tablespoons nonfat chocolate or caramel sauce.

Bamboozlers

4 squares (1 ounce each)
   unsweetened chocolate,
   coarsely chopped
½ cup butter or margarine
2 large eggs
1¼ cups granulated sugar
1 teaspoon vanilla
½ cup all-purpose flour
½ teaspoon salt
1 white baking bar (6 ounces),
   cut into ¼-inch pieces
½ cup coarsely chopped walnuts
   (optional)
Powdered sugar for garnish

WHITE CHOCOLATE CHUNK BROWNIES

Makes about 16 brownies

Preheat oven to 350°F. Melt unsweetened chocolate and butter in small, heavy saucepan over low heat, stirring constantly; set aside. Beat eggs in large bowl; gradually add granulated sugar, beating at medium speed about 4 minutes until very thick and lemon colored. Beat in chocolate mixture and vanilla. Beat in flour and salt just until blended. Stir in baking bar pieces and walnuts. Spread evenly into greased 8-inch square baking pan. Bake 30 minutes or until edges begin to pull away from sides of pan and center is set. Remove pan to wire rack; cool completely. Cut into 2-inch squares. Sprinkle with powdered sugar, if desired.

White Chocolate Chunk Brownies

1 package (4 ounces) BAKER'S®
GERMAN'S® Sweet
Chocolate
¼ cup (½ stick) margarine or
butter
¾ cup sugar
2 eggs
1 teaspoon vanilla
½ cup all-purpose flour
½ cup chopped nuts

GERMAN SWEET CHOCOLATE BROWNIES

Makes about 16 brownies

HEAT oven to 350°F.

MICROWAVE chocolate and margarine in large microwavable bowl on HIGH (100% power) 2 minutes or until margarine is melted. **Stir until chocolate is completely melted.**

STIR sugar into melted chocolate mixture. Mix in eggs and vanilla until well blended. Stir in flour and nuts. Spread into greased 8-inch square pan.

BAKE for 25 minutes or until toothpick inserted into center comes out with fudgy crumbs. **Do not overbake.** Cool in pan; cut into squares.

PREP TIME: 10 MINUTES
BAKE TIME: 25 MINUTES

BROWNIE LAYER

 ½ **cup butter or margarine**

 ⅓ **cup unsweetened cocoa**

 1 **cup sugar**

 2 **eggs, slightly beaten**

 1 **teaspoon vanilla**

 ½ **cup all-purpose flour**

 ½ **teaspoon baking powder**

 ¼ **teaspoon salt**

CHEESE LAYER

 ¾ **cup (6 ounces) SARGENTO®**
    Part-Skim Ricotta Cheese

 ¼ **cup sugar**

 1 **egg, slightly beaten**

 2 **tablespoons butter or**
    margarine, softened

 1 **tablespoon all-purpose flour**

 ½ **teaspoon vanilla**

RICOTTA CHEESE BROWNIES

Makes 16 brownies

For brownie layer, preheat oven to 350°F. Melt butter in small saucepan; remove from heat. Stir in cocoa; cool. In large bowl of electric mixer, beat sugar, eggs and vanilla on medium speed until light and fluffy. In small bowl, stir together flour, baking powder and salt. Add to egg mixture; beat until blended. Add cocoa mixture; beat until thoroughly combined. Reserve 1 cup batter; spread remaining batter into greased 8-inch square baking pan.

For cheese layer, in small bowl of electric mixer, beat ricotta cheese, sugar, egg, butter, flour and vanilla on medium speed until well blended. Spread over brownie layer in pan. Drop teaspoonfuls of reserved brownie batter over cheese mixture; spread batter with spatula to cover cheese mixture. Bake 40 minutes. Cool.

DECADENT BLONDE BROWNIES

Makes about 2 dozen brownies

½ cup butter or margarine,
    softened
¾ cup granulated sugar
¾ cup packed light brown sugar
2 large eggs
2 teaspoons vanilla
1½ cups all-purpose flour
1 teaspoon baking powder
½ teaspoon salt
1 package (10 ounces)
    semisweet chocolate chunks
1 jar (3½ ounces) macadamia
    nuts, coarsely chopped

Preheat oven to 350°F. Beat butter, granulated sugar and brown sugar in large bowl with electric mixer at medium speed until light and fluffy. Beat in eggs and vanilla. Add combined flour, baking powder and salt. Stir until well blended. Stir in chocolate chunks and macadamia nuts. Spread evenly into greased 13×9-inch baking pan.

Bake 25 to 30 minutes or until golden brown. Remove pan to wire rack; cool completely. Cut into 3¼×1½-inch bars.

EASY DOUBLE CHOCOLATE CHIP BROWNIES

Makes 2 dozen brownies

2 cups (12-ounce package)
    NESTLÉ® TOLL HOUSE®
    Semi-Sweet Chocolate
    Morsels, divided
½ cup (1 stick) butter or
    margarine, cut into pieces
3 eggs
1¼ cups all-purpose flour
1 cup granulated sugar
¼ teaspoon baking soda
1 teaspoon vanilla extract
½ cup chopped nuts

MELT *1 cup* morsels and butter in large, heavy saucepan over low heat; stir until smooth. Remove from heat. Add eggs; stir well. Add flour, sugar, baking soda and vanilla; stir well. Stir in *remaining 1 cup* morsels and nuts. Spread into greased 13×9-inch baking pan.

BAKE in preheated 350°F oven for 18 to 22 minutes or until wooden pick inserted in center comes out with fudgy crumbs. Cool completely. Cut into 2-inch squares.

Decadent Blonde Brownies

½ cup butter or margarine,
  softened
¼ cup peanut butter
1 cup packed light brown sugar
½ cup granulated sugar
3 eggs
1 teaspoon vanilla
2 cups all-purpose flour
2 teaspoons baking powder
⅛ teaspoon salt
1 cup chocolate-flavored syrup
½ cup coarsely chopped salted
  mixed nuts

MARBLED PEANUT BUTTER BROWNIES

Makes about 2 dozen brownies

Preheat oven to 350°F. Lightly grease 13×9-inch pan. Beat butter and peanut butter in large bowl until blended; stir in sugars. Beat in eggs, one at a time, until batter is light. Blend in vanilla. Combine flour, baking powder and salt in small bowl. Stir into creamed mixture. Spread half the batter evenly in prepared pan. Spread syrup over top. Spoon remaining batter over syrup. Swirl with knife or spatula to create a marbled effect. Sprinkle chopped nuts over top. Bake 35 to 40 minutes or until lightly browned. Cool in pan on wire rack. Cut into 2-inch squares.

Marbled Peanut Butter Brownies

6 squares (1 ounce each)
    semisweet chocolate,
    coarsely chopped
1 tablespoon freeze dried coffee
1 tablespoon boiling water
¾ cup all-purpose flour
¾ teaspoon ground cinnamon
½ teaspoon baking powder
¼ teaspoon salt
½ cup sugar
¼ cup butter or margarine,
    softened
3 large eggs, divided
¼ cup whipping cream
1 teaspoon vanilla
¾ cup flaked coconut, divided
½ cup semisweet chocolate
    chips, divided

COCONUT CROWNED CAPPUCCINO BROWNIES

Makes 16 brownies

1. Preheat oven to 350°F. Grease 8-inch square baking pan; set aside.

2. Melt chocolate squares in small, heavy saucepan over low heat, stirring constantly; set aside. Dissolve coffee in boiling water in small cup; set aside.

3. Place flour, cinnamon, baking powder and salt in small bowl; stir to combine.

4. Beat sugar and butter in large bowl with electric mixer at medium speed until light and fluffy. Beat in 2 eggs, 1 at a time, scraping down side of bowl after each addition. Beat in chocolate mixture and coffee mixture until well combined. Add flour mixture. Beat at low speed until well blended. Spread batter evenly into prepared baking pan.

5. For topping, combine cream, remaining 1 egg and vanilla in small bowl; mix well. Stir in ½ cup coconut and ¼ cup chips. Spread evenly over brownie base; sprinkle with remaining ¼ cup coconut and chips. Bake 30 to 35 minutes or until coconut is browned and center is set. Remove pan to wire rack; cool completely. Cut into 2-inch squares.

6. Store tightly covered at room temperature or freeze up to 3 months.

Coconut Crowned Cappuccino Brownies

½ cup butter or margarine

3 squares (1 ounce each)
    bittersweet chocolate*

2 eggs

1 cup sugar

1 teaspoon vanilla

¾ cup all-purpose flour

¼ teaspoon baking powder
    Dash salt

½ cup sliced or slivered almonds

½ cup raspberry preserves

1 cup (6 ounces) milk chocolate
    chips

Bittersweet chocolate is available in specialty food stores. One square unsweetened chocolate plus 2 squares semisweet chocolate may be substituted.

RASPBERRY FUDGE BROWNIES

Makes 16 brownies

Preheat oven to 350°F. Butter and flour 8-inch square pan. Melt butter and bittersweet chocolate in small heavy saucepan over low heat. Remove from heat; cool. Beat eggs, sugar and vanilla in large bowl until light. Beat in chocolate mixture. Stir in flour, baking powder and salt until just blended. Spread ¾ batter into prepared pan; sprinkle almonds over top. Bake 10 minutes. Remove from oven; spread preserves over almonds. Carefully spoon remaining batter over preserves, smoothing top. Bake 25 to 30 minutes or just until top feels firm. Remove from oven; sprinkle chocolate chips over top. Let stand a few minutes until chips melt; spread evenly over brownies. Cool completely in pan on wire rack. When chocolate is set, cut into 2-inch squares.

C H O C O L A T E   T I P

A continental classiness is attached to the dark or bittersweet chocolate. Many premium dark chocolate bars are imported from Belgium, Switzerland and Italy.

Raspberry Fudge Brownies

1¼ cups all-purpose flour
½ teaspoon baking soda
¼ teaspoon salt
¾ cup granulated sugar
½ cup (1 stick) butter or
     margarine
2 tablespoons water
1½ cups (10-ounce package)
     NESTLÉ® TOLL HOUSE®
     Mint-Chocolate Morsels,
     divided
1 teaspoon vanilla extract
2 eggs

MOIST AND MINTY BROWNIES

Makes about 16 brownies

COMBINE flour, baking soda and salt in small bowl; set aside. Combine sugar, butter and water in medium saucepan. Bring just to a boil over medium heat, stirring constantly; remove from heat. Add *1 cup* morsels and vanilla; stir until smooth. Add eggs one at a time, stirring well after each addition. Stir in flour mixture and *remaining* morsels. Spread into greased 9-inch square baking pan.

BAKE in preheated 350°F oven for 20 to 30 minutes or until center is set. Cool (center will sink) in pan on wire rack.

1 cup (6 ounces) semisweet
     chocolate chips
6 tablespoons butter or
     margarine
2 eggs
⅓ cup honey
1 teaspoon vanilla
½ cup all-purpose flour
½ teaspoon baking powder
     Dash salt
1 cup chopped walnuts

HONEY BROWNIES

Makes 16 brownies

Preheat oven to 350°F. Butter 8-inch square pan. Melt chocolate and butter in medium heavy saucepan over low heat. Remove from heat; cool slightly. Stir in eggs, honey and vanilla. Combine flour, baking powder and salt in small bowl. Stir into chocolate mixture with walnuts. Spread batter evenly into prepared pan. Bake 20 to 25 minutes or just until center feels springy. Cool in pan on wire rack. Cut into 2-inch squares.

¾ **cup butter**

2 **squares (1 ounce each)**
   semisweet chocolate,
   coarsely chopped

2 **squares (1 ounce each)**
   unsweetened chocolate,
   coarsely chopped

1¾ **cups sugar**

1 **tablespoon instant espresso**
   powder or instant coffee
   granules

3 **eggs**

¼ **cup orange-flavored liqueur**

2 **teaspoons grated orange peel**

1 **cup all-purpose flour**

1 **package (12 ounces)**
   semisweet chocolate chips

2 **tablespoons shortening**

1 **orange for garnish**

ORANGE CAPPUCCINO BROWNIES

Makes about 2 dozen brownies

1. Preheat oven to 350°F. Grease 13×9-inch pan.

2. Melt butter, chopped semisweet chocolate and unsweetened chocolate in large heavy saucepan over low heat, stirring constantly. Stir in granulated sugar and espresso powder. Remove from heat. Cool slightly.

3. Beat in eggs, 1 at a time, with wire whisk. Whisk in liqueur and orange peel. Beat flour into chocolate mixture until just blended. Spread batter evenly into prepared pan. Bake 25 to 30 minutes or until center is just set. Remove pan to wire rack.

4. Meanwhile, melt chocolate chips and shortening in small, heavy saucepan over low heat, stirring constantly.

5. Immediately after removing brownies from oven, spread hot chocolate mixture over warm brownies. Cool completely in pan on wire rack. Cut into 2-inch squares. Garnish, if desired.

6. To make orange peel garnish, remove thin strips of peel from orange using citrus zester. Tie strips into knots or twist into spirals.

4 squares (1 ounce each)
    unsweetened chocolate
1 cup sugar
¼ cup Prune Purée (recipe
    follows) or prepared prune
    butter
3 egg whites
1 to 2 tablespoons instant
    espresso coffee powder
1 teaspoon baking powder
1 teaspoon salt
1 teaspoon vanilla
½ cup all-purpose flour
    Powdered sugar (optional)

CHOCOLATE ESPRESSO BROWNIES

Makes 36 brownies

Preheat oven to 350°F. Coat 8-inch square baking pan with vegetable cooking spray. In small heavy saucepan, melt chocolate over very low heat, stirring until melted and smooth. Remove from heat; cool. In mixer bowl, beat chocolate, sugar, prune purée, egg whites, espresso powder, baking powder, salt and vanilla at medium speed until well blended; mix in flour. Spread batter evenly into prepared pan. Bake in center of oven about 30 minutes until pick inserted into center comes out clean. Cool completely in pan on wire rack. Dust with powdered sugar. Cut into 1⅓-inch squares.

FAVORITE RECIPE FROM CALIFORNIA FRUIT BOARD

PRUNE PURÉE : Combine 1⅓ cups (8 ounces) pitted prunes and 6 tablespoons hot water in container of food processor or blender. Pulse on and off until prunes are finely chopped and smooth. Store leftovers in a covered container in the refrigerator for up to two months.

Chocolate Espresso Brownies

RICH 'N' CREAMY BROWNIE BARS

Makes 48 bars

BROWNIES

> 1 package DUNCAN HINES®
>   Double Fudge Brownie Mix
> 2 eggs
> ⅓ cup water
> ¼ cup CRISCO® Oil or CRISCO®
>   PURITAN® Canola Oil
> ½ cup chopped pecans

TOPPING

> 1 package (8 ounces) cream
>   cheese, softened
> 2 eggs
> 1 pound (3½ cups)
>   confectioners' sugar
> 1 teaspoon vanilla extract

1. Preheat oven to 350°F. Grease bottom of 13×9×2-inch pan.

2. **For brownies,** combine brownie mix, contents of fudge packet from Mix, 2 eggs, water and oil in large bowl. Stir with spoon until well blended, about 50 strokes. Stir in pecans. Spread evenly into prepared pan.

3. **For topping,** beat cream cheese in large bowl at medium speed with electric mixer until smooth. Beat in 2 eggs, confectioners' sugar and vanilla extract until smooth. Spread evenly over brownie mixture. Bake at 350°F for 45 to 50 minutes or until edges and top are golden brown and shiny. Cool completely. Refrigerate until well chilled. Cut into bars.

Rich 'n' Creamy Brownie Bars

4 squares BAKER'S®
   Unsweetened Chocolate
¾ cup (1½ sticks) margarine or
   butter
2 cups sugar
3 eggs
1 teaspoon vanilla
1 cup all-purpose flour
1 cup BAKER'S® Semi-Sweet
   Real Chocolate Chips
1½ cups chopped nuts
1 package caramels (48)
⅓ cup evaporated milk

CARAMEL–LAYERED BROWNIES

Makes about 24 brownies

HEAT oven to 350°F.

MICROWAVE chocolate and margarine in large microwavable bowl on HIGH 2 minutes or until margarine is melted. **Stir until chocolate is completely melted.**

STIR sugar into melted chocolate mixture. Mix in eggs and vanilla until well blended. Stir in flour. Remove 1 cup of batter; set aside. Spread remaining batter into greased 13×9-inch pan. Sprinkle with chips and 1 cup of the nuts.

MICROWAVE caramels and milk in same bowl on HIGH 4 minutes, stirring after 2 minutes. Stir until caramels are completely melted and smooth. Spoon over chips and nuts, spreading to edges of pan. Gently spread reserved batter over caramel mixture. Sprinkle with the remaining ½ cup nuts.

BAKE for 40 minutes or until toothpick inserted into center comes out with fudgy crumbs. **Do not overbake.** Cool in pan; cut into squares.

PREP TIME: 20 MINUTES
BAKE TIME: 40 MINUTES

Caramel-Layered Brownies

EXQUISITE BROWNIE TORTE

Makes 12 to 16 servings

FILLING

1 package (3 ounces) cream
    cheese, softened
⅓ cup confectioners' sugar
¼ teaspoon almond extract
1 package whipped topping mix
½ cup milk

RASPBERRY SAUCE

1 tablespoon cornstarch
2 tablespoons cold water
1 package (10 ounces) frozen
    raspberries in light syrup,
    thawed
2 tablespoons seedless red
    raspberry jam
¼ teaspoon lemon juice
1 tablespoon Amaretto
    (optional)
1 package DUNCAN HINES®
    Walnut Brownie Mix
½ pint fresh raspberries
½ cup fresh blueberries
    Mint leaves, for garnish

1. For filling, combine cream cheese, confectioners' sugar and almond extract in large bowl. Beat at medium speed with electric mixer until softened and blended. Add whipped topping mix and milk. Beat at high speed for 4 minutes or until mixture thickens and forms peaks. Cover. Refrigerate for 2 to 3 hours or until thoroughly chilled.

2. For raspberry sauce, dissolve cornstarch in water in medium saucepan. Add thawed raspberries, raspberry jam and lemon juice. Cook on medium heat until mixture comes to a boil. Remove from heat; add Amaretto, if desired. Push mixture through sieve into small bowl to remove seeds. Refrigerate for 2 to 3 hours or until thoroughly chilled.

3. Preheat oven to 350°F. Line 9-inch springform pan with aluminum foil. Grease bottom of foil.

4. Prepare brownies following package directions for basic recipe. Spread in prepared pan. Bake for 35 to 37 minutes or until set. Cool completely. Remove from pan. Peel off aluminum foil.

5. To assemble, place brownie torte on serving plate. Spread chilled filling over top of brownie. Place ¼ cup raspberry sauce in small resealable plastic bag. Snip pinpoint hole in bottom corner of bag. Drizzle sauce in three concentric rings one inch apart. Draw toothpick in straight lines from center to edge through topping and sauce to form web design. Arrange fresh raspberries and blueberries in center. Garnish with mint leaves. Serve with remaining sauce.

1 package DUNCAN HINES®
    Fudge Brownie Mix
1 egg
⅓ cup water
⅓ cup CRISCO® Oil or CRISCO®
    PURITAN® Canola Oil
¾ cup semi-sweet chocolate
    chips
½ cup chopped pecans

CINDY'S FUDGY BROWNIES

Makes 24 Brownies

1. Preheat oven to 350°F. Grease bottom of 13×9×2-inch pan.

2. Combine brownie mix, egg, water and oil in large bowl. Stir with spoon until well blended, about 50 strokes. Stir in chocolate chips. Spread in pan. Sprinkle with pecans. Bake at 350°F for 25 to 28 minutes or until set. Cool completely. Cut into bars.

TIP: Overbaking brownies will cause them to become dry. Follow the recommended baking times given in recipes closely.

¼ cup (½ stick) light corn oil
    spread
2 egg whites
1 egg
¾ cup sugar
⅔ cup all-purpose flour
⅓ cup HERSHEY'S Cocoa
½ teaspoon baking powder
¼ teaspoon salt
    Mocha Glaze (recipe follows)

MINI BROWNIE CUPS

Makes 2 dozen brownie cups

Heat oven to 350°F. Line 24 small muffin cups (1¾ inches in diameter) with paper bake cups or spray with vegetable cooking spray. In small saucepan over low heat, melt corn oil spread; cool slightly. In small mixer bowl, beat egg whites and egg on medium speed of electric mixer until foamy; gradually add sugar, beating until slightly thickened and light in color. In small bowl, stir together flour, cocoa, baking powder and salt; add gradually to egg mixture, beating until blended. Gradually add corn oil spread; beat just until blended. Fill muffin cups ⅔ full with batter.

Bake 15 to 18 minutes or until wooden pick inserted in centers comes out clean. Remove from pans to wire racks. Cool completely. Drizzle Mocha Glaze over tops of brownie cups. Let stand until set. Store, covered, at room temperature.

MOCHA GLAZE

¼ cup powdered sugar
¾ teaspoon HERSHEY'S Cocoa
¼ teaspoon powdered instant coffee
2 teaspoons hot water
¼ teaspoon vanilla extract

In small bowl, stir together powdered sugar and cocoa. Dissolve coffee in water; add to sugar mixture, stirring until well blended. Stir in vanilla.

Mini Brownie Cups

2 jars (10 ounces each)
   maraschino cherries with
   stems
Cherry liqueur (optional)*
4 squares BAKER'S®
   Unsweetened Chocolate
¾ cup (1½ sticks) margarine or
   butter
2 cups granulated sugar
4 eggs
1 teaspoon vanilla
1 cup all-purpose flour
   Chocolate Fudge Filling
      (page 152)
½ cup powdered sugar

*For liqueur-flavored cherries, drain
liquid from cherries. Do not remove
cherries from jars. Refill jars with
liqueur to completely cover cherries;
cover tightly. Let stand at least
24 hours for best flavor.

BROWNIE BON BONS

Makes about 48 bon bons

HEAT oven to 350°F.

MICROWAVE chocolate and margarine in large microwavable bowl on HIGH 2 minutes or until margarine is melted. **Stir until chocolate is completely melted.**

STIR granulated sugar into melted chocolate mixture. Mix in eggs and vanilla until well blended. Stir in flour. Fill greased 1¾×1-inch muffin cups ⅔ full with batter.

BAKE for 20 minutes or until toothpick inserted into center comes out with fudgy crumbs. **Do not overbake.** Cool slightly in muffin pans; loosen edges with tip of knife. Remove from pans. Turn each brownie onto wax paper-lined tray while warm. Make ½-inch indentation into top of each brownie with end of wooden spoon. Cool.

PREPARE Chocolate Fudge Filling. Drain cherries, reserving liquid or liqueur. Let cherries stand on paper towels to dry. Combine powdered sugar with enough reserved liquid to form a thin glaze.

SPOON or pipe about 1 teaspoon Chocolate Fudge Filling into indentation of each brownie. Gently press cherry into filling. Drizzle with powdered sugar glaze.

PREP TIME: 1 HOUR
BAKE TIME: 20 MINUTES

continued on page 152

Brownie Bon Bons

Brownie Bon Bons continued from
page 150

CHOCOLATE FUDGE FILLING

1 package (3 ounces) PHILADELPHIA BRAND® cream cheese, softened

1 teaspoon vanilla

$^1/_4$ cup corn syrup

3 squares BAKER'S® Unsweetened Chocolate, melted and cooled

1 cup powdered sugar

BEAT cream cheese and vanilla in small bowl until smooth. Slowly pour in corn syrup, beating until well blended. Add chocolate; beat until smooth. Gradually add powdered sugar, beating until well blended and smooth.

Makes about 1 cup

CHOCOLATE TIP

Chocolate had its serious side. During World War II home economists prepared air-raid-shelter menus to be printed in newspapers and magazines.

These menus were written to suggest no fuss quick-energy meals. Then considered a universal food, chocolate was almost always included.

⅓ cup cold water

1 (15-ounce package) brownie
    mix

¼ cup oil

1 egg

1 (8-ounce package)
    PHILADELPHIA BRAND®
    Cream Cheese, softened

¼ cup sugar

1 egg

1 teaspoon vanilla
    Strawberry slices
    Banana slices

2 (1-ounce squares) **BAKER'S®**
    Semi-Sweet Chocolate,
    melted

BANANA BERRY BROWNIE PIZZA

Makes 10 to 12 servings

▨ Preheat oven to 350°F.

▨ Bring water to boil.

▨ Mix together brownie mix, boiled water, oil and egg in large bowl until well blended.

▨ Pour into greased and floured 12-inch pizza pan.

▨ Bake 25 minutes.

▨ Beat cream cheese, sugar, egg and vanilla in small mixing bowl at medium speed with electric mixer until well blended. Pour over crust.

▨ Bake 15 minutes. Cool. Top with fruit; drizzle with chocolate. Garnish with mint leaves, if desired.

PREP TIME: 35 MINUTES

COOK TIME: 40 MINUTES

Microwave Tip: To melt chocolate, place unwrapped chocolate squares in small bowl. Microwave on HIGH 1 to 2 minutes or until almost melted. Stir until smooth.

PEANUT BUTTER BROWNIE CUPS

Makes 24 brownie cups

BROWNIE CUPS

> 1 package DUNCAN HINES®
>   Double Fudge Brownie Mix
> 2 eggs
> ⅓ cup water
> ¼ cup CRISCO® Oil or CRISCO®
>   PURITAN® Canola Oil

TOPPING

> ⅓ cup sugar
> ⅓ cup light corn syrup
> ½ cup peanut butter

CHOCOLATE GLAZE

> ¾ cup semi-sweet chocolate
>   chips
> 3 tablespoons butter or
>   margarine
> 1 tablespoon light corn syrup
> 3 tablespoons chopped peanuts,
>   for garnish

1. Preheat oven to 350°F. Place 24 (2-inch) foil liners on baking sheets.

2. **For brownie cups,** combine brownie mix, fudge packet from Mix, eggs, water and oil in large bowl. Stir with spoon until well blended, about 50 strokes. Place 2 level measuring tablespoons batter in each foil liner. Bake 20 to 22 minutes or until firm. Cool completely.

3. **For topping,** combine sugar and ⅓ cup corn syrup in small heavy saucepan. Bring to a boil on medium heat. Stir in peanut butter. Drop by rounded teaspoonfuls onto each brownie cup.

4. **For chocolate glaze,** combine chocolate chips, butter and 1 tablespoon corn syrup in small heavy saucepan. Cook, stirring constantly, on low heat until melted. Spoon 1 rounded teaspoonful chocolate glaze onto peanut butter topping. Sprinkle with chopped peanuts. Refrigerate 15 minutes or until chocolate is firm.

Peanut Butter Brownie Cups

2 pints strawberries, cut in half

2 tablespoons sugar

1 teaspoon vanilla

2 (9-inch) layers ONE BOWL® Chocolate Cake (page 162)

Semi-Sweet Chocolate Glaze (recipe follows)

3½ cups (8 ounces) COOL WHIP® Whipped Topping, thawed

Chocolate-dipped strawberries (optional)

CHOCOLATE STRAWBERRY SHORTCAKE

Makes 12 servings

MIX strawberries, sugar and vanilla. Spoon ½ of the strawberry mixture on 1 cake layer. Drizzle with ½ the chocolate glaze; top with ½ the whipped topping. Repeat layers. Garnish with chocolate-dipped strawberries, if desired. Refrigerate.

PREP TIME: 15 MINUTES

SEMI-SWEET CHOCOLATE GLAZE

3 squares BAKER'S® Semi-Sweet Chocolate

3 tablespoons water

1 tablespoon margarine or butter

1 cup powdered sugar

½ teaspoon vanilla

MICROWAVE chocolate, water and margarine in large microwavable bowl on HIGH 1 to 2 minutes or until chocolate is almost melted, stirring once. Stir until chocolate is completely melted.

STIR in sugar and vanilla until smooth. For thinner glaze, add ½ to 1 teaspoon additional water.

Makes about ¾ cup

PREP TIME: 10 MINUTES

Chocolate Strawberry Shortcake

1 package DUNCAN HINES®
   Moist Deluxe Dark
   Chocolate Fudge Cake Mix
½ gallon brick vanilla ice cream

FUDGE SAUCE
   1 can (12 ounces) evaporated
      milk
1¼ cups sugar
   4 squares (1 ounce each)
      unsweetened chocolate
¼ cup butter or margarine
1½ teaspoons vanilla extract
¼ teaspoon salt
   Whipped cream and
      maraschino cherries, for
      garnish

HOT FUDGE SUNDAE CAKE

Makes 12 to 16 servings

1. Preheat oven to 350°F. Grease and flour 13×9×2-inch pan. Prepare, bake and cool cake following package directions.

2. Remove cake from pan. Split cake in half horizontally. Place bottom layer back in pan. Cut ice cream into even slices and place evenly over bottom cake layer (use all the ice cream). Place remaining cake layer over ice cream. Cover and freeze.

3. **For fudge sauce,** combine evaporated milk and sugar in medium saucepan. Stir constantly on medium heat until mixture comes to a rolling boil. Boil and stir for 1 minute. Add unsweetened chocolate and stir until melted. Beat over medium heat until smooth. Remove from heat. Stir in butter, vanilla and salt.

4. Cut cake into serving squares. For each serving, place cake square on plate; spoon hot fudge sauce on top. Garnish with whipped cream and maraschino cherry.

TIP: Fudge sauce may be prepared ahead and refrigerated in tightly sealed jar. Reheat when ready to serve.

Hot Fudge Sundae Cake

2 cups flour

²⁄₃ cup unsweetened cocoa

1¼ teaspoons baking soda

¼ teaspoon baking powder

3 eggs

1²⁄₃ cups sugar

1 teaspoon vanilla

1 cup HELLMANN'S® or BEST
     FOODS® Real or Light
     Mayonnaise or Low Fat
     Mayonnaise Dressing

1⅓ cups water

CHOCOLATE MAYONNAISE CAKE

Makes one 9-inch layer cake

Preheat oven to 350°F. Grease and flour bottoms of 2 (9×1½-inch) round cake pans. In medium bowl, combine flour, cocoa, baking soda and baking powder; set aside. In large bowl with mixer at high speed, beat eggs, sugar and vanilla, scraping bowl occasionally, 3 minutes or until smooth and creamy. Reduce speed to low; beat in mayonnaise until blended. Add flour mixture in 4 additions alternately with water, beginning and ending with flour mixture. Pour into prepared pans.

Bake 30 to 35 minutes or until cake springs back when touched lightly in center. Cool in pans on wire racks 10 minutes. Remove from pans; cool completely on racks. Fill and frost as desired.

Chocolate Mayonnaise Cake

6 squares BAKER'S® Semi-Sweet
Chocolate

¾ cup (1½ sticks) margarine or
butter

1½ cups sugar

3 eggs

2 teaspoons vanilla

2½ cups all-purpose flour

1 teaspoon baking soda

¼ teaspoon salt

1½ cups water

ONE BOWL® CHOCOLATE CAKE

Makes 12 servings

HEAT oven to 350°F.

MICROWAVE chocolate and margarine in large
microwavable bowl on HIGH 2 minutes or until margarine
is melted. **Stir until chocolate is completely melted.**

STIR sugar into melted chocolate mixture until well
blended. Beat in eggs, one at a time, with electric mixer
until completely mixed. Add vanilla. Add ½ cup of the
flour, the baking soda and salt; mix well. Beat in the
remaining 2 cups flour alternately with water until smooth.
Pour into 2 greased and floured 9-inch layer pans.

BAKE for 35 minutes or until toothpick inserted into
center comes out clean. Cool in pans 10 minutes. Remove
from pans to cool on wire racks. Fill and frost as desired.

PREP TIME: 15 MINUTES
BAKE TIME: 35 MINUTES

BLACK FOREST CAKE (AS SHOWN): Mix 1 can (21 ounces)
cherry pie filling, drained, and ¼ cup cherry liqueur (or
½ teaspoon almond extract). Spoon evenly over 1 cake
layer, reserving a few cherries for garnish, if desired. Spread
1½ cups thawed COOL WHIP® Whipped Topping over
cherries; top with second cake layer. Frost top and sides
with additional 2 cups whipped topping. Garnish as
desired. Refrigerate.

One Bowl® Chocolate Cake

1½ **cups all-purpose flour**
1 **cup sugar**
¼ **cup HERSHEY'S Cocoa**
1 **teaspoon baking soda**
½ **teaspoon salt**
1 **cup water**
¼ **cup vegetable oil**
1 **tablespoon white vinegar**
1 **teaspoon vanilla extract**
2 **cups peeled, sliced fresh peaches, divided**

PEACHY CHOCOLATE CAKE

Makes 12 servings

Heat oven to 350°F. Grease and flour two 8-inch round baking pans. In large bowl, stir together flour, sugar, cocoa, baking soda and salt. Add water, oil, vinegar and vanilla. Beat with wire whisk or spoon just until batter is smooth and ingredients are well blended. Pour into prepared pans. Bake 20 to 25 minutes or until wooden pick inserted in center comes out clean. Cool 10 minutes; remove from pans to wire racks. Cool completely. Just before serving, place one cake layer on serving plate; arrange 1 cup of the peaches on layer. Top with second cake layer and remaining 1 cup peaches. Cut into slices; serve immediately.

CHOCOLATE TIP

Milk chocolate is pure chocolate mixed with sugar, extra cocoa butter and milk solids. Milk chocolate can not be used interchangeably with other chocolates because the presence of milk changes its melting and cooking characteristics.

1 package DUNCAN HINES®
   Angel Food Cake Mix
16 large marshmallows
½ cup milk
1 package (11½ ounces) milk
   chocolate chips
1 pint whipping cream
¼ cup semisweet chocolate chips
1½ teaspoons CRISCO®
   all-vegetable shortening

CHOCOLATE ANGEL FOOD DESSERT

Makes 12 to 16 servings

1. Preheat oven to 350°F. Prepare, bake and cool cake following package directions.

2. Melt marshmallows and milk in heavy saucepan over low heat. Remove from heat; stir in milk chocolate chips until melted. Cool to room temperature. Beat whipping cream in large bowl until stiff peaks form. Fold cooled chocolate mixture into whipped cream. Refrigerate until spreading consistency.

3. To assemble, split cake horizontally into 3 even layers. Place 1 cake layer on serving plate. Spread with one-fourth of frosting. Repeat with second layer. Top with third layer. Frost sides and top with remaining frosting. Refrigerate.

4. For drizzle, place semisweet chocolate chips and shortening in 1-cup glass measuring cup. Microwave at MEDIUM (50% power) for 1 minute. Stir until smooth. Drizzle melted chocolate around outer top edge of cake, allowing mixture to run down sides unevenly. Refrigerate until ready to serve.

TIP: For even layers, measure cake with ruler. Divide in 3 equal layers. Mark with toothpicks. Cut layers with serrated knife using toothpicks as guide.

1 package (18.25 ounces)
    chocolate fudge cake mix
    with pudding
3 eggs
¾ cup water
½ cup KAHLÚA® Liqueur
⅓ cup vegetable oil
1 can (16 ounces) vanilla or
    chocolate frosting
1 can (21 ounces) cherry filling
    and topping
    Chocolate shavings or
    chocolate sprinkles for
    garnish (optional)

KAHLÚA® BLACK FOREST CAKE

Makes 1 (9-inch) cake

Preheat oven to 350°F. Grease and flour 2 (9-inch) cake pans; set aside. In large mixer bowl, prepare cake mix according to package directions, using eggs, water, Kahlúa® and oil. Pour batter into prepared pans. Bake 25 to 35 minutes or until toothpick inserted in center comes out clean. Cool cake in pans 10 minutes; turn layers out onto wire racks to cool completely.

Place one cake layer bottom side up on serving plate. Spread thick layer of frosting in circle, 1½ inches around outer edge of cake. Spoon half of cherry filling into center of cake layer to frosting edge. Top with second cake layer, bottom side down. Repeat with frosting and remaining cherry filling. Spread remaining frosting around side of cake. Decorate with chocolate shavings or sprinkles, if desired.

Kahlúa® Black

1 package DUNCAN HINES®
 Moist Deluxe Devil's Food
 Cake Mix
12 bars (1.4 ounces each)
 chocolate covered toffee
 bars, divided
3 cups whipping cream, chilled

CHOCOLATE TOFFEE CRUNCH FANTASY

Makes 12 servings

1. Preheat oven to 350°F. Grease and flour 10-inch tube pan.

2. Prepare, bake and cool cake following package directions. Split cake horizontally into three layers; set aside. Chop 11 candy bars into pea-size pieces (see Tip). Whip cream until stiff peaks form. Fold candy pieces into whipped cream.

3. To assemble, place one split cake layer on serving plate. Spread 1½ cups whipped cream mixture on top. Repeat with remaining layers and whipped cream mixture. Frost sides and top with remaining filling. Chop remaining candy bar coarsely. Sprinkle over top. Refrigerate until ready to serve.

Tip: To quickly chop toffee candy bars, place a few bars in food processor fitted with steel blade. Pulse several times until pea-size pieces form. Repeat with remaining candy bars.

Chocolate Toffee Crunch Fantasy

1 cup water

½ cup Prune Purée (recipe, page 183) or prepared prune butter

3 egg whites

1½ teaspoons vanilla

1 cup plus 2 tablespoons all-purpose flour

1 cup plus 2 tablespoons granulated sugar

¾ cup unsweetened cocoa powder

1½ teaspoons baking powder

¼ teaspoon baking soda

¼ teaspoon salt

⅔ cup no-sugar-added raspberry spread

¼ cup raspberry or orange-flavored liqueur

1½ cups crushed fresh raspberries

Additional fresh raspberries, for garnish

Powdered sugar

1½ cups low fat nondairy whipped topping

CHOCOLATE–RASPBERRY LAYER CAKE

Makes 12 servings

Preheat oven to 350°F. Coat two 8-inch round layer cake pans with vegetable cooking spray. In mixer bowl, beat water, prune purée, egg whites and vanilla at medium speed until well blended. In medium bowl, combine flour, granulated sugar, cocoa, baking powder, baking soda and salt; mix into prune purée mixture until well blended. Spread batter equally in prepared pans. Bake in center of oven about 20 minutes until pick inserted into centers comes out clean. Cool in pans 10 minutes; remove from pans to wire racks to cool completely. Refrigerate 1 hour.

Using serrated knife, carefully split each layer horizontally. Place one layer on cake plate. In small bowl, mix raspberry spread with liqueur; spread about one third of mixture over cake layer. Spread with ½ cup crushed raspberries. Repeat layers two more times. Place remaining cake layer on top, cut side down, and press gently. Cover and refrigerate several hours or overnight. Garnish with whole raspberries and dust with powdered sugar. Cut into wedges. Dollop each wedge with 2 tablespoons whipped topping.

FAVORITE RECIPE FROM CALIFORNIA PRUNE BOARD.

Chocolate-Raspberry Layer Cake

2 cups sugar

1¾ cups all-purpose flour

¾ cup HERSHEY'S Cocoa or
   HERSHEY'S European
   Style Cocoa

1½ teaspoons baking powder

1½ teaspoons baking soda

1 teaspoon salt

2 eggs

1 cup milk

½ cup vegetable oil

2 teaspoons vanilla extract

1 cup boiling water

One-Bowl Buttercream
   Frosting (recipe follows)

DEEP DARK CHOCOLATE CAKE

Makes 8 to 10 servings

Heat oven to 350°F. Grease and flour two 9-inch round cake pans.* In large mixer bowl, stir together sugar, flour, cocoa, baking powder, baking soda and salt. Add eggs, milk, oil and vanilla; beat on medium speed of electric mixer 2 minutes. Stir in water. (Batter will be thin.) Pour batter evenly into prepared pans. Bake 30 to 35 minutes or until wooden pick inserted in center comes out clean. Cool 10 minutes; remove from pans to wire racks. Cool completely. Prepare One-Bowl Buttercream Frosting; spread between layers and over top and side of cake.

One 13×9×2-inch baking pan may be substituted for 9-inch cake pans. Prepare as directed. Bake 35 to 40 minutes. Cool completely in pan on wire rack. Frost as desired.

ONE-BOWL BUTTERCREAM FROSTING

6 tablespoons butter or margarine, softened

2⅔ cups powdered sugar

½ cup HERSHEY'S Cocoa

⅓ cup milk

1 teaspoon vanilla extract

In small mixer bowl, beat butter. Blend in powdered sugar and cocoa alternately with milk, beating well after each addition until smooth and of spreading consistency. Blend in vanilla. Add additional milk, if needed.

Deep Dark Chocolate Cake

2 cups (15 ounces) SARGENTO®
    Part-Skim Ricotta Cheese
¼ cup sugar
3 tablespoons orange liqueur
⅓ cup finely chopped mixed
    candied fruit
¼ cup chopped almonds
1¼ cups semisweet mini
    chocolate chips, divided
1 prepared pound cake
    (10¾ ounces)
1 teaspoon instant coffee
    dissolved in ¼ cup boiling
    water
6 tablespoons unsalted butter or
    margarine, cut into 8 pieces,
    chilled
Chopped almonds (optional)

CASSATA

Makes 12 servings

Combine ricotta cheese, sugar and liqueur in large bowl; beat until light and fluffy, about 3 minutes. Fold in candied fruit, almonds and ¼ cup chocolate chips; set aside.

Cut pound cake in half horizontally using sharp serrated knife. Cut each half again horizontally. Place top of pound cake, top side down, on serving platter. Spread one-third of the ricotta mixture evenly over cake. Repeat procedure twice. Top with remaining cake layer; press lightly to compact layers. Cover with plastic wrap; refrigerate at least 2 hours.

Meanwhile, place remaining 1 cup chocolate chips and coffee mixture in top of double boiler set over hot, not boiling, water. Stir constantly until chocolate is melted. Add butter pieces, 1 at a time, stirring constantly, until all butter is added and melted. Remove from heat; refrigerate until spreading consistency, about 2 to 2½ hours.

Spread top and sides of cake with frosting. Sprinkle top with chopped almonds, if desired.

TIP: Cake can be made 1 day in advance, covered with plastic wrap and refrigerated. Let stand at room temperature about 30 minutes before slicing.

CRUST:

> ⅔ cup all-purpose flour
> 2 tablespoons sugar
> ⅓ cup margarine or butter
> ½ cup toasted finely chopped almonds

TOPPING:

> 4 squares BAKER'S® Semi-Sweet Chocolate
> ½ cup (1 stick) margarine or butter
> ½ cup sugar
> ⅓ cup heavy cream
> 2 eggs, lightly beaten
> ½ teaspoon vanilla
> 1 can (16 ounces) pear halves, drained and thinly sliced
> ½ cup toasted coarsely chopped almonds

CHOCOLATE ALMOND PEAR TORTE

Makes 8 servings

HEAT oven to 375°F.

MIX flour and 2 tablespoons sugar in medium bowl; cut in ⅓ cup margarine until mixture resembles coarse crumbs. Stir in finely chopped almonds. Press firmly onto bottom of 9-inch springform pan or onto bottom and sides of 9-inch pie plate. Bake for 10 minutes.

MICROWAVE chocolate and ½ cup margarine in large microwavable bowl on HIGH 2 minutes or until margarine is melted. **Stir until chocolate is completely melted.**

STIR in ½ cup sugar and cream, mixing well. Stir in eggs and vanilla. Pour over crust.

ARRANGE pear slices over filling. Sprinkle filling with coarsely chopped almonds. Bake for 35 to 40 minutes or until toothpick inserted into center comes out almost clean. (Center may be slightly soft.) Cool on wire rack. Refrigerate.

PREP TIME: 30 MINUTES
BAKE TIME: 45 TO 50 MINUTES

1½ cups chocolate wafer crumbs
(approximately 30 wafers)

6 tablespoons butter or
margarine, melted

2 tablespoons sugar

2 tablespoons butter or
margarine

2 tablespoons sugar

1 cup chopped almonds

½ cup cold water

¾ cup sugar

1 (8-ounce) package
PHILADELPHIA BRAND®
Cream Cheese, softened

6 (1-ounce) squares BAKER'S®
Semi-Sweet Chocolate,
melted

1½ cups whipping cream,
whipped

1 pint premium coffee ice cream

LAYERED FROZEN MOUSSE TORTE

Makes 10 to 12 servings

■ Preheat oven to 350°F. Stir together crumbs,
6 tablespoons butter and 2 tablespoons sugar in small
bowl; press onto bottom and 2 inches up sides of 9-inch
springform pan. Bake 10 minutes.

■ Meanwhile, melt 2 tablespoons butter in medium skillet
over medium heat. Stir in 2 tablespoons sugar and almonds;
cook 1 minute. Reduce heat to low; continue cooking
almonds until golden brown, stirring constantly. Spread hot
almond mixture over hot crust; press down lightly. Cool.

■ Stir together water and ¾ cup sugar in small saucepan.
Bring to boil; reduce heat to medium. Simmer 3 minutes.

■ Beat cream cheese in large bowl at medium speed with
electric mixer until smooth. Gradually add sugar mixture.
Blend in chocolate. Fold in whipped cream.

■ Spread half of chocolate mixture over almond mixture.
Refrigerate remaining chocolate mixture. Place springform
pan in freezer 2 hours or until chocolate is firm.

■ Soften ice cream to spreading consistency. Spread over
frozen chocolate layer; top with remaining chocolate
mixture. Freeze several hours or overnight. Let stand at room
temperature 10 to 15 minutes before serving. Garnish with
whipped cream, chocolate lace and coffee beans, if desired.

PREP TIME: 40 MINUTES PLUS FREEZING

Layered Frozen Mousse Torte

1 package DUNCAN HINES®
   Moist Deluxe Devil's Food
   Cake Mix
1 can (21 ounces) cherry pie
   filling
¼ teaspoon almond extract
1 container (8 ounces) frozen
   whipped topping, thawed
   and divided
¼ cup toasted sliced almonds,
   for garnish (see Tip)

CHOCOLATE CHERRY TORTE

Makes 12 to 16 servings

1. Preheat oven to 350°F. Grease and flour two 9-inch round cake pans.

2. Prepare, bake and cool cake following package directions for basic recipe. Combine cherry pie filling and almond extract in small bowl. Stir until blended.

3. To assemble, place one cake layer on serving plate. Spread with 1 cup whipped topping, then half the cherry pie filling mixture. Top with second cake layer. Spread with remaining pie filling to within 1½ inches of cake edge. Decorate cake edge with remaining whipped topping. Garnish with sliced almonds.

TIP: To toast almonds, spread in a single layer on baking sheet. Bake at 325°F for 4 to 6 minutes or until fragrant and golden.

Chocolate Cherry Torte

1 package DUNCAN HINES®
    Moist Deluxe Dark
    Chocolate Fudge Cake Mix
Egg substitute product equal
    to 3 eggs
1¼ cups water
½ cup CRISCO® PURITAN®
    Canola Oil

RASPBERRY SAUCE
1 package (12 ounces) frozen
    dry pack raspberries,
    thawed, drained and juice
    reserved
½ cup sugar
2 teaspoons cornstarch
½ teaspoon grated lemon peel
1 can (29 ounces) sliced peaches
    in lite syrup, drained

FUDGE CAKE WITH MELBA TOPPING

Makes 20 servings

1. Preheat oven to 350°F. Grease and flour 13×9×2-inch pan.

2. FOR CAKE: Combine cake mix, egg substitute, water and oil in large bowl. Beat at medium speed with electric mixer for 2 minutes. Pour into pan. Bake at 350°F for 35 to 40 minutes or until toothpick inserted in center comes out clean. Cool completely.

3. FOR SAUCE: Combine reserved raspberry juice, sugar, cornstarch and lemon peel in medium saucepan. Bring to a boil. Reduce heat and cook until thickened, stirring constantly. Stir in reserved raspberries. Cool.

4. Cut cake into serving squares. Place several peach slices on top of cake square. Spoon raspberry sauce over peaches and cake. Serve immediately.

TIP: To separate juice from raspberries in one step, allow berries to thaw at room temperature in a strainer placed over a bowl.

Fudge Cake with Melba Topping

Apple Topping (recipe
  follows)
1 cup all-purpose flour
⅔ cup sugar
¼ cup HERSHEY'S Cocoa or
  HERSHEY'S European
  Style Cocoa
1 teaspoon baking powder
½ teaspoon salt
¾ cup water
⅔ cup shortening
1 egg
1 teaspoon vanilla extract
  Whipped topping or ice cream
  (optional)

APPLE PIE CHOCOLATE BROWNIE CAKE

Makes 8 to 10 servings

Prepare Apple Topping. Heat oven to 375°F. Grease and flour 9-inch square baking pan. In medium bowl, stir together flour, sugar, cocoa, baking powder and salt. Add water, shortening, egg and vanilla; beat until smooth and well blended. Spread into prepared pan. *Carefully* spoon prepared topping over chocolate batter to within ½ inch of edges. *Do not stir.* Bake 35 to 40 minutes or until chocolate is set and cakelike. Cool completely in pan on wire rack. Serve with whipped topping, if desired. Garnish as desired.

APPLE TOPPING

1 can (20 ounces) apple pie filling
½ teaspoon lemon juice
½ teaspoon ground cinnamon

In small bowl, stir together apple pie filling, lemon juice and cinnamon.

CHOCOLATE TIP

Hershey's European Style Cocoa is Dutch-process cocoa. It has been treated with an alkaline solution to help neutralize cocoa's natural acidity.

Dutch-process cocoa is a darker, more mellow-flavored cocoa.

1½ cups graham cracker crumbs

3 tablespoons sugar

¼ cup Prune Purée (recipe
   follows) or prepared prune
   butter

¼ cup semisweet miniature
   chocolate chips

2 cans (20 ounces each) cherry
   pie filling

CHERRY-CHOCOLATE CRUMBLE

Makes 8 servings

Preheat oven to 375°F. In medium bowl, mix crumbs and sugar. Cut in prune purée with pastry blender until mixture resembles coarse crumbs. Mix in chocolate chips. Spread pie filling evenly in 8-inch square baking dish or pan; cover evenly with crumb mixture. Bake in center of oven about 20 minutes until cherries are bubbly and topping is lightly browned. Cool on wire rack 15 minutes. Serve warm, topped with fat free vanilla frozen yogurt, if desired.

PRUNE PURÉE: Combine 1⅓ cups (8 ounces) pitted prunes and 6 tablespoons hot water in container of food processor or blender. Pulse on and off until prunes are finely chopped and smooth. Store leftovers in a covered container in the refrigerator for up to two months.

FAVORITE RECIPE FROM CALIFORNIA PRUNE BOARD

1½ cups FLEISCHMANN'S®
   Margarine, divided
4 eggs
1 cup unsweetened cocoa,
   divided
1½ cups all-purpose flour
2 cups sugar
¼ teaspoon salt
1¼ cups PLANTERS® Pecans,
   chopped
3 cups miniature marshmallows
35 NILLA® Wafers
1 (1-pound) box confectioners'
   sugar
½ cup milk
½ teaspoon vanilla extract

MISSISSIPPI NILLA MUD CAKE

Makes 24 servings

Preheat oven to 350°F. In large bowl, with electric mixer at medium speed, beat 1 cup margarine, eggs and ½ cup cocoa until well combined. Blend in flour, sugar, salt and pecans. Spread batter into greased 13×9×2-inch baking pan. Bake at 350°F for 30 to 35 minutes or until cake pulls away from sides of pan.

Sprinkle marshmallows over hot cake; return to oven for 2 minutes or until marshmallows are slightly puffed. Arrange wafers over marshmallow layer.

In medium bowl, with electric mixer at medium speed, beat remaining ½ cup margarine, confectioners' sugar, remaining ½ cup cocoa, milk and vanilla until smooth; spread immediately over wafer layer. Cool cake completely on wire rack. Cut into squares to serve.

Mississippi Nilla Mud Cake

CAKE

1¾ cups granulated sugar

¾ CRISCO® Stick or ¾ cup CRISCO all-vegetable shortening

2 eggs

2 tablespoons HERSHEY'S Cocoa

1 tablespoon McCORMICK®/ SCHILLING® Pure Vanilla Extract

¼ teaspoon salt

½ cup buttermilk or sour milk*

1 teaspoon baking soda

2½ cups all-purpose flour

1 cup cola soft drink (not diet)

FROSTING

1 box (1 pound) confectioners' sugar (3½ to 4 cups)

6 tablespoons or more cola soft drink (not diet)

¼ cup HERSHEY'S Cocoa

¼ CRISCO® Stick or ¼ cup CRISCO all-vegetable shortening

1 cup chopped pecans, divided

To sour milk: Combine 1½ teaspoons white vinegar plus enough milk to equal ½ cup. Stir. Wait 5 minutes.

CHOCA-COLA CAKE

Makes 12 to 16 servings

1. Heat oven to 350°F. Line bottom of 13×9×2-inch baking pan with waxed paper.

2. For cake, combine granulated sugar and ¾ cup shortening in large bowl. Beat at medium speed of electric mixer 1 minute. Add eggs. Beat until blended. Add 2 tablespoons cocoa, vanilla and salt. Beat until blended.

3. Combine buttermilk and baking soda in small bowl. Add to creamed mixture. Beat until blended. Reduce speed to low. Add flour alternately with 1 cup cola, beginning and ending with flour, beating at low speed after each addition until well blended. Pour into pan.

4. Bake at 350°F for 30 to 35 minutes or until cake begins to pull away from sides of pan. Cool 10 minutes before removing from pan. Invert cake on wire rack. Remove waxed paper. Cool completely. Place cake on serving tray.

5. For frosting, combine confectioners' sugar, 6 tablespoons cola, ¼ cup cocoa and ¼ stick shortening in medium bowl. Beat at low, then medium speed until blended, adding more cola, if necessary, until of desired spreading consistency. Stir in ½ cup nuts. Frost top and sides of cake. Sprinkle remaining nuts over top of cake. Let stand at least 1 hour before serving.

Note: Flavor of cake improves if made several hours or a day before serving.

Choca-Cola Cake

CAKE

> 1 cup water
> ½ cup Prune Purée (recipe follows) or prepared prune butter
> 3 egg whites
> 1½ teaspoons vanilla
> 1 cup plus 2 tablespoons all-purpose flour
> 1 cup plus 2 tablespoons granulated sugar
> ¾ cup unsweetened cocoa powder
> 1½ teaspoons baking powder
> ¼ teaspoon baking soda
> ¼ teaspoon salt

ICING

> 2½ cups powdered sugar
> ¼ cup unsweetened cocoa powder
> ¼ cup low fat (1%) milk
> Fresh raspberries and mint sprig, for garnish

LOW FAT DEVIL'S CHOCOLATE FUDGE CAKE

Makes 9 servings

Preheat oven to 350°F. Coat 9-inch square baking pan with vegetable cooking spray. To make cake, in mixer bowl, beat water, prune purée, egg whites and vanilla until well blended. Add flour, granulated sugar, ¾ cup cocoa, baking powder, baking soda and salt; mix well. Spread batter evenly in prepared pan. Bake in center of oven about 30 minutes until pick inserted into center comes out clean. Cool completely in pan on wire rack.

To make icing, in small mixer bowl, beat powdered sugar, ¼ cup cocoa and milk until smooth. Spread on cake. Garnish with raspberries and mint. Cut cake into 3-inch squares.

PRUNE PURÉE: Combine 1⅓ cups (8 ounces) pitted prunes and 6 tablespoons hot water in container of food processor or blender. Pulse on and off until prunes are finely chopped and smooth. Store leftovers in a covered container in the refrigerator for up to two months.

TIP: Unsweetened cocoa powder provides rich chocolate flavor with less fat than other baking chocolates because most of the cocoa butter has been removed.

FAVORITE RECIPE FROM CALIFORNIA PRUNE BOARD

Low Fat Devil's Chocolate Fudge Cake

6 cups sifted powdered sugar

1¼ cups unsweetened cocoa powder

1 cup Prune Purée (recipe follows) or prepared prune butter, divided

½ cup cold water

¾ teaspoon salt

¼ to ½ teaspoon peppermint extract

3 eggs

1 tablespoon instant espresso coffee powder *or* 2 tablespoons instant coffee granules

1½ cups all-purpose flour

1½ teaspoons baking soda

¾ cup boiling water

1 tablespoon nonfat milk

TOUCH O' MINT CHOCOLATE FUDGE CAKE

Makes 15 servings

Preheat oven to 350°F. Coat 13×9-inch baking pan with vegetable cooking spray. In mixer bowl, mix sugar, cocoa, ⅔ cup prune purée, cold water, salt and peppermint extract on low speed 30 seconds; beat on high speed until mixture is very smooth, 1 to 2 minutes. Transfer 2 cups of sugar mixture to another mixer bowl. Cover remaining 4 cups sugar mixture for frosting; set aside. Add remaining ⅓ cup prune purée, eggs and espresso powder to 2 cups sugar mixture; beat on medium speed 30 seconds. Beat on high 2 minutes until well blended. Combine flour and baking soda; mix into sugar mixture just until blended. Slowly add boiling water, mixing 1 minute more. (Cake batter will be thick and fluffy.) Spread batter evenly into prepared pan. Bake in center of oven about 35 minutes until barely springy to the touch and pick inserted into center comes out almost clean. (**Do not overbake.**) Cool completely in pan on wire rack. Meanwhile, mix milk and reserved sugar mixture until well blended; spread over cake. Cut into squares.

PRUNE PURÉE: Combine 1⅓ cups (8 ounces) pitted prunes and 6 tablespoons hot water in container of food processor or blender. Pulse on and off until prunes are finely chopped and smooth. Store leftovers in a covered container in the refrigerator for up to two months.

FAVORITE RECIPE FROM **CALIFORNIA PRUNE BOARD**

2¼ cups chocolate wafer cookie
    crumbs, divided
½ cup sugar, divided
½ cup (1 stick) margarine or
    butter, melted
1 package (8 ounces)
    PHILADELPHIA BRAND®
    Cream Cheese, cubed,
    softened
1 tub (12 ounces) COOL WHIP®
    Whipped Topping, thawed,
    divided
2 cups boiling water
1 package (8-serving size) *or*
    2 packages (4-serving size)
    JELL-O® Brand Orange
    Flavor Gelatin
½ cup cold water
    Ice cubes
    Rectangular or oval-shaped
    sandwich cookies
    Decorator icings
    Candy corn and pumpkins

GRAVEYARD TREAT

Makes 15 to 18 servings

MIX 2 cups of the cookie crumbs, ¼ cup of the sugar and the melted margarine with fork in 13×9-inch baking pan until crumbs are well moistened. Press firmly onto bottom of pan to form crust. Refrigerate.

BEAT cream cheese and remaining ¼ cup sugar in medium bowl with wire whisk until smooth. Gently stir in ½ of the whipped topping. Spread evenly over crust.

STIR boiling water into gelatin in medium bowl 2 minutes or until completely dissolved. Mix cold water and ice cubes to make 1½ cups. Add to gelatin; stir until slightly thickened (consistency of unbeaten egg whites). Remove any remaining ice. Spoon gelatin over cream cheese layer.

REFRIGERATE 3 hours or until firm. Spread remaining whipped topping over gelatin just before serving; sprinkle with remaining ¼ cup cookie crumbs. Decorate sandwich cookies with icings to make "tombstones." Stand tombstones on top of dessert with candies to resemble a graveyard. Cut into squares to serve.

1 package DUNCAN HINES®
Moist Deluxe Devil's Food
Cake Mix

FILLING
1 cup evaporated milk
1 cup granulated sugar
24 large marshmallows
1 package (14 ounces) flaked
coconut

TOPPING
½ cup butter or margarine
¼ cup plus 2 tablespoons milk
⅓ cup unsweetened cocoa
1 pound confectioners' sugar
(3½ to 4 cups)
1 teaspoon vanilla extract
¾ cup sliced almonds

CHOCOLATE CONFECTION CAKE

Makes 20 to 24 servings

1. Preheat oven to 350°F. Grease and flour 15½×10½×1-inch jelly-roll pan.

2. Prepare cake following package directions for original recipe. Pour into pan. Bake at 350°F for 20 to 25 minutes or until toothpick inserted in center comes out clean.

3. **For filling,** combine evaporated milk and granulated sugar in large saucepan. Bring mixture to a boil. Add marshmallows and stir until melted. Stir in coconut. Spread on warm cake.

4. **For topping,** combine butter, milk and cocoa in medium saucepan. Stir on low heat until butter is melted. Add confectioners' sugar and vanilla extract, stirring until smooth. Stir in almonds (see Tip). Pour over filling. Spread evenly to edges. Cool completely.

TIP: For a pretty presentation, sprinkle the ¾ cup almond slices over topping instead of stirring almonds into topping.

Chocolate Confection Cake

1¾ cups all-purpose flour
⅓ cup unsweetened cocoa
powder
2 teaspoons baking powder
1 teaspoon baking soda
½ teaspoon salt
1 cup granulated sugar
¾ cup MOTT'S® Natural Apple
Sauce
½ cup skim milk
4 egg whites
1 teaspoon vanilla extract
Powdered sugar
¾ cup marshmallow topping
½ cup frozen light nondairy
whipped topping, thawed
2 tablespoons chopped unsalted
peanuts
Powdered sugar (optional)
Fresh red currants (optional)
Mint leaves (optional)

ROCKY ROAD CAKE

Makes 14 servings

1. Preheat oven to 350°F. Line 15½×10½-inch jelly-roll pan with waxed paper.

2. In medium bowl, sift together flour, cocoa, baking powder, baking soda and salt.

3. In large bowl, whisk together granulated sugar, apple sauce, milk, egg whites and vanilla.

4. Add flour mixture to apple sauce mixture; stir until well blended. Pour batter into prepared pan.

5. Bake 12 to 15 minutes or until top springs back when lightly touched. Immediately invert onto clean, lint-free dish towel sprinkled with powdered sugar; peel off waxed paper. Trim edges of cake. Starting at narrow end, roll up cake and towel together. Cool completely on wire rack.

6. In small bowl, whisk marshmallow topping until softened. Gently fold in whipped topping.

7. Unroll cake; spread with marshmallow mixture to within ½ inch of edges of cake. Sprinkle peanuts over marshmallow mixture. Reroll cake; place, seam side down, on serving plate. Cover; refrigerate 1 hour before slicing. Sprinkle with powdered sugar and garnish with currants and mint leaves, if desired, just before serving. Cut into 14 slices. Refrigerate leftovers.

Rocky Road Cake

3 large eggs, separated

½ cup sugar

5 ounces semi-sweet chocolate, melted

⅓ cup water

1 teaspoon vanilla

¾ cup all-purpose flour

1 teaspoon baking powder

½ teaspoon baking soda

¼ teaspoon salt

Unsweetened cocoa

½ cup seedless strawberry or raspberry jam

2 pints strawberry ice cream, softened

STRAWBERRY CHOCOLATE ROLL

Makes 8 to 12 servings

Preheat oven to 350°F. Line 15×10-inch jelly-roll pan with foil, extending foil 1 inch over ends of pan; grease and flour foil.

Beat egg yolks and sugar in medium bowl until light and fluffy. Beat in melted chocolate. Add water and vanilla. Mix until smooth. Sift flour, baking powder, baking soda and salt together. Add to chocolate mixture.

Using clean beaters and large bowl, beat egg whites until soft peaks form. Gently fold in chocolate mixture. Pour into prepared pan.

Bake 8 to 9 minutes or until wooden pick inserted center comes out clean. Carefully loosen sides of cake from foil. Invert cake onto clean towel sprinkled with cocoa. Peel off foil. Starting at short end, roll warm cake, jelly-roll fashion with towel inside. Cool cake completely.

Unroll cake; remove towel. Spread cake with jam. Spread cake with ice cream, leaving ¼-inch border. Roll up cake; wrap tightly in plastic wrap or foil. Freeze. Allow cake to stand at room temperature 10 minutes before cutting and serving.

Strawberry Chocolate Roll

¾ cup granulated sugar

2 eggs

3 egg whites

¼ cup Prune Purée (page 190) or prepared prune butter

¼ cup coffee-flavored liqueur, divided

2 tablespoons instant coffee granules

1 cup all-purpose flour

¼ cup unsweetened cocoa powder, divided

¼ teaspoon salt

Powdered sugar

1½ cups low fat non-dairy whipped topping

Additional low fat non-dairy whipped topping and chocolate covered coffee beans, for garnish

MOCHA CAKE ROLL WITH CREAMY CHOCOLATE FILLING

Makes 12 servings

Preheat oven to 425°F. Coat 13×9×2-inch baking pan with vegetable cooking spray. Line pan with parchment or waxed paper; coat paper with vegetable cooking spray. In top of double boiler or bowl set over simmering water, combine granulated sugar, eggs and egg whites. Beat at high speed with portable electric mixer until tripled in volume, about 5 minutes. Beat in prune purée, 2 tablespoons liqueur and coffee granules until well blended; remove from heat. In medium bowl, combine flour, 2 tablespoons cocoa and salt. Sift flour mixture over egg mixture; gently fold in just until blended. Spread batter evenly in prepared pan. Bake in center of oven 10 minutes or until springy to the touch.

Meanwhile, lay cloth tea towel on work surface; dust with powdered sugar. When cake is done, immediately loosen edges and invert onto towel. Gently peel off paper. Roll cake up in towel from narrow end. Place seam side down on wire rack; cool completely. Gently unroll cake; brush with remaining 2 tablespoons liqueur. Combine whipped topping with remaining 2 tablespoons cocoa. Spread evenly over cake. Reroll without towel. Place seam side down on serving plate. Dust with powdered sugar. Garnish with additional whipped topping and coffee beans.

FAVORITE RECIPE FROM CALIFORNIA PRUNE BOARD

Mocha Cake Roll With Creamy Chocolate Filling

CHOCOLATE CRUNCH CAKE

Makes 8 servings

- 1 cup Wheat CHEX® brand cereal, crushed to ½ cup
- 1 cup Corn CHEX® brand cereal, crushed to ½ cup
- ¼ cup chopped walnuts
- ¼ cup packed brown sugar
- 1 package (9 ounces) devil's food cake mix, divided
- ¼ cup (½ stick) margarine or butter, melted
- 1 egg, beaten
- ½ cup sour cream
- 1 teaspoon instant coffee crystals
- ¼ cup semi-sweet chocolate pieces
- Whipped topping, optional
- Maraschino cherries, optional
- Shaved chocolate, optional

Preheat oven to 350°F. Lightly grease 4-cup fluted ovenproof pan. Combine cereals, nuts, brown sugar and 2 tablespoons cake mix in small bowl; mix well. Add margarine, stirring until well combined. Press ¾ cup of mixture onto bottom and side of prepared pan. Combine remaining cake mix, egg, sour cream and coffee in large bowl. Beat 4 minutes or until well blended. Stir in chocolate pieces. Pour into prepared pan; top with remaining cereal mixture. Bake 30 to 35 minutes or until wooden toothpick inserted in center comes out clean. Cool in pan 10 minutes. Remove from pan; cool completely. Garnish with whipped topping and cherries or chocolate if desired.

CHOCOLATE TIP

For a special touch, top with chocolate shavings. To shave chocolate, place a block of chocolate on a cutting board. Using a paring knife, skim the edge of the block to form small slivers.

1 package (about 18 ounces)
    lemon cake mix
⅓ cup poppy seed
⅓ cup milk
3 eggs
1 container (8 ounces) plain
    lowfat yogurt
1 teaspoon freshly grated lemon
    peel
Chocolate Citrus Glaze (recipe
    follows)

CHOCOLATE GLAZED CITRUS POPPY SEED CAKE

Makes 12 servings

Heat oven to 350°F. Grease and flour 12-cup fluted tube pan or 10-inch tube pan. In large mixer bowl, combine cake mix, poppy seed, milk, eggs, yogurt and lemon peel; beat until well blended. Pour batter into prepared pan. Bake 40 to 45 minutes or until wooden pick inserted in center comes out clean. Cool 20 minutes; remove from pan to wire rack. Cool completely. Prepare Chocolate Citrus Glaze; spoon over cake, allowing glaze to run down sides.

CHOCOLATE CITRUS GLAZE

  2 tablespoons butter or margarine
  2 tablespoons HERSHEY'S Cocoa or HERSHEY'S
    European Style Cocoa
  2 tablespoons water
  1 tablespoon orange-flavored liqueur (optional)
  ½ teaspoon orange extract
1¼ to 1½ cups powdered sugar

In small saucepan over medium heat, melt butter. With whisk, stir in cocoa and water until mixture thickens slightly. Remove from heat; stir in liqueur, if desired, orange extract and 1¼ cups powdered sugar. Whisk until smooth. If glaze is too thin, whisk in remaining ¼ cup powdered sugar. Use immediately.

ALMOND FUDGE BANANA CAKE

Makes 16 to 20 servings

3 extra-ripe, medium DOLE®
Bananas, peeled

1½ cups sugar

½ cup margarine, softened

3 eggs

3 tablespoons amaretto liqueur
or ½ to 1 teaspoon almond
extract

1 teaspoon vanilla

1⅓ cups all-purpose flour

⅓ cup unsweetened cocoa
powder

1 teaspoon baking soda

½ teaspoon salt

½ cup DOLE® Chopped
Almonds, toasted, ground

BANANA CHOCOLATE GLAZE

1 extra-ripe, small DOLE®
Banana, puréed

1 square (1 ounce) semisweet
chocolate, melted

■ Mash bananas.

■ Beat sugar and margarine until light and fluffy. Beat in eggs, liqueur and vanilla.

■ Combine flour, cocoa, baking soda and salt. Stir in almonds. Add to beaten sugar mixture alternately with bananas. Beat well.

■ Turn batter into greased 10-inch Bundt pan. Bake in 350°F oven 45 to 50 minutes or until wooden toothpick inserted in center comes out nearly clean and cake pulls away from sides of pan. Cool 10 minutes. Remove cake from pan to wire rack to cool completely. Drizzle glaze over top and down sides of cake.

■ For Banana Chocolate Glaze, with wire whisk, beat puréed banana into melted chocolate.

Almond Fudge Banana Cake

STREUSEL

1 package DUNCAN HINES®
Moist Deluxe Devil's Food
Cake Mix, divided
1 cup finely chopped pecans
2 tablespoons brown sugar
2 teaspoons ground cinnamon

CAKE

3 eggs
1⅓ cups water
½ cup CRISCO® Oil or CRISCO®
PURITAN® Canola Oil

TOPPING

1 container (8 ounces) frozen
whipped topping, thawed
3 tablespoons sifted
unsweetened cocoa
Chopped pecans, for garnish
(optional)
Chocolate curls, for garnish
(optional)

CHOCOLATE STREUSEL CAKE

Makes 12 to 16 servings

1. Preheat oven to 350°F. Grease and flour 10-inch Bundt pan.

2. **For streusel,** combine 2 tablespoons cake mix, 1 cup pecans, brown sugar and cinnamon. Set aside.

3. **For cake,** combine remaining cake mix, eggs, water and oil in large bowl. Beat at medium speed with electric mixer for 2 minutes. Pour two-thirds of batter into pan. Sprinkle with reserved streusel. Pour remaining batter evenly over streusel. Bake at 350°F for 55 to 60 minutes or until toothpick inserted in center comes out clean. Cool in pan 25 minutes. Invert onto serving plate. Cool completely.

4. **For topping,** place whipped topping in medium bowl. Fold in cocoa until blended. Spread on cooled cake. Garnish with chopped pecans and chocolate curls, if desired. Refrigerate until ready to serve.

TIP: For chocolate curls, warm chocolate in microwave oven at HIGH (100% power) for 5 to 10 seconds. Make chocolate curls by holding a sharp vegetable peeler against flat side of chocolate block and bringing blade toward you. Apply firm pressure for thicker, more open curls or light pressure for tighter curls.

Chocolate Streusel Cake

2 tablespoons dark rum

4 single graham cracker squares

5 eggs, separated

2 cups powdered sugar

1 teaspoon grated orange peel

¼ teaspoon cream of tartar

3½ cups finely ground toasted California walnuts

¼ cup grated semisweet chocolate

6 squares (1 ounce each) semisweet chocolate

6 tablespoons butter or margarine

1 tablespoon honey

California walnut halves for garnish

WALNUT HOLIDAY CAKE

Makes 16 servings

In small bowl, pour rum over graham crackers. When crackers are softened, mash with fork.

In large bowl, beat egg yolks at medium speed until lemon colored. Add sugar and orange peel; beat at high speed until thick, about 3 minutes. Beat cracker mixture into yolk mixture. In separate large bowl, beat egg whites with cream of tartar at high speed until stiff, but not dry, peaks form. Gently fold beaten whites, ground walnuts and grated chocolate into yolk mixture.

Grease 9-inch springform pan; line bottom with waxed paper and grease again. Pour batter into prepared pan. Bake in preheated 350°F oven 45 to 50 minutes or until wooden toothpick inserted in center comes out clean and small cracks appear on surface. Let cool completely in pan on wire rack. Remove side of springform pan. Invert cake onto serving plate; remove bottom of pan and waxed paper. Place strips of waxed paper under cake to cover plate.

In top of double boiler set over simmering water, melt chocolate squares and butter; stir to blend. Stir in honey. Pour chocolate mixture over cake; let stand until slightly cool. Spread over top and side of cake. Remove waxed paper strips. Garnish, if desired. When firm, cut into thin wedges.

FAVORITE RECIPE FROM **WALNUT MARKETING BOARD**

½ cup butter

8 ounces (8 squares) semi-sweet baking chocolate, divided

3 extra-large eggs

¾ cup granulated sugar

1¼ cups finely ground walnuts or pecans

2 tablespoons all-purpose flour

5 tablespoons KAHLÚA®, divided

1 teaspoon vanilla

Sifted powdered sugar

Strawberries, chocolate nonpareils candy or coffee beans for garnish (optional)

KAHLÚA® CHOCOLATE DECADENCE

Makes 1 (9-inch) cake

Preheat oven to 325°F. In small saucepan over medium heat, or in microwave-safe bowl on HIGH (100% power), melt butter and 6 ounces chocolate, stirring until blended. Remove from heat; cool. In large bowl, beat eggs and granulated sugar on high speed of electric mixer about 3 minutes or until light and lemon-colored. Stir together walnuts and flour; gradually beat into egg mixture.

Stir 3 tablespoons Kahlúa® and vanilla into cooled chocolate mixture; gradually beat into egg mixture until well combined. Pour batter into 9-inch springform pan. Bake 35 to 45 minutes or until top is set. Cool cake in pan.

Remove side of pan; place cake on serving plate. Sprinkle top with powdered sugar. Melt remaining 2 ounces semi-sweet baking chocolate as previously directed. Stir together melted chocolate and remaining 2 tablespoons Kahlúa; drizzle over cake. Decorate with strawberries, chocolate nonpareils candy or coffee beans if desired.

Kahlúa® Chocolate Decadence

1¼ cups sugar, divided

⅔ cup unsweetened cocoa
    powder

2 tablespoons all-purpose flour

¾ cup nonfat milk

5 ounces semisweet chocolate
    chips (about ¾ cup)

¼ cup Prune Purée (page 218) or
    prepared prune butter

1 egg

1 egg yolk

1 teaspoon vanilla

2 egg whites

⅛ teaspoon cream of tartar

    Raspberry Sauce (recipe
    follows)

1½ cups low fat non-dairy
    whipped topping

    Fresh raspberries and mint
    leaves, for garnish

A LIGHTER CHOCOLATE DECADENCE

Makes 12 servings

Preheat oven to 350°F. Line 9-inch round layer cake pan with parchment paper or waxed paper; coat with vegetable cooking spray. In medium saucepan, combine 1 cup sugar, cocoa and flour. Slowly whisk in milk until blended. Bring to a simmer over low heat, stirring constantly. Place chocolate chips in large bowl; pour in hot mixture, stirring until chocolate melts. Whisk in prune purée, egg, egg yolk and vanilla until blended. Set aside to cool. In mixer bowl, beat egg whites with cream of tartar until foamy. Gradually beat in remaining ¼ cup sugar until stiff peaks form. Fold half the egg white mixture into cooled chocolate mixture; fold in remaining egg white mixture. Pour into prepared pan. Bake in center of oven 30 to 35 minutes until puffy and center is set but still moist. (**Do not overbake.**) Cool completely in pan on wire rack. (**Cake will sink as it cools.**) Remove from pan. Wrap securely; chill 24 hours before serving. Prepare Raspberry Sauce. Cut dessert into wedges; serve with Raspberry Sauce and whipped topping. Garnish with raspberries and mint leaves.

RASPBERRY SAUCE: Purée 1 package (12 ounces) thawed frozen raspberries in blender; strain to remove seeds. Sweeten to taste with sugar.   *Makes 1 cup*

FAVORITE RECIPE FROM CALIFORNIA PRUNE BOARD

A Lighter Chocolate Decadence

CHOCOLATE INTENSITY

Makes one 9-inch cake

CAKE

- 1 package (8 ounces) NESTLÉ® Unsweetened Chocolate Baking Bars
- 1½ cups granulated sugar
- ½ cup butter, softened
- 3 eggs
- 2 teaspoons vanilla extract
- ⅔ cup all-purpose flour
- Powdered sugar (optional)

COFFEE CRÈME ANGLAISE SAUCE

- 4 egg yolks
- ⅓ cup granulated sugar
- 1 tablespoon freeze dried instant coffee
- 1½ cups milk
- 1 teaspoon vanilla extract

FOR CAKE, in small heavy saucepan over low heat, melt baking bars, stirring until smooth. Remove from heat; cool to lukewarm. In small mixer bowl, beat sugar, butter, eggs and vanilla for about 4 minutes or until thick and pale yellow. Beat in melted chocolate. Gradually beat in flour. Spread into greased 9-inch springform pan. Bake in preheated 350°F oven for 25 to 28 minutes. Wooden pick inserted in center will be moist. Cool in pan on wire rack for 15 minutes. Remove side of pan; cool completely. Sprinkle with powdered sugar.

FOR COFFEE CRÈME ANGLAISE SAUCE, in small bowl, whisk egg yolks. In medium saucepan, combine sugar and coffee; stir in milk. Cook over medium heat, stirring constantly, until mixture comes to a simmer. Remove from heat. Gradually whisk ½ of hot milk mixture into yolks; return to saucepan. Continue cooking, stirring constantly for 3 to 4 minutes or until mixture is slightly thickened. Strain into small bowl; stir in vanilla. Cover with plastic wrap; refrigerate until chilled.

To serve, cut cake into 10 or 12 servings. Serve with 3 to 4 tablespoons sauce.

Chocolate Intensity

1 package DUNCAN HINES®
   Moist Deluxe Dark
   Chocolate Fudge Cake Mix
1 package (7 ounces) pure
   almond paste
½ cup seedless red raspberry
   jam
3 cups semi-sweet chocolate
   chips
½ cup plus 1 tablespoon
   CRISCO® all-vegetable
   shortening

CHOCOLATE PETITS FOURS

Makes 24 to 32 servings

1. Preheat oven to 350°F. Grease and flour 13×9×2-inch pan.

2. Prepare, bake and cool cake following package directions for basic recipe. Remove from pan. Cover and store overnight (see Tip). Level top of cake. Trim ¼-inch strip of cake from all sides. (Be careful to make straight cuts.) Cut cake into small squares, rectangles or triangles with serrated knife. Cut round and heart shapes with 1½- to 2-inch cookie cutters. Split each individual cake horizontally into two layers.

3. For filling, cut almond paste in half. Roll half the paste between two sheets of waxed paper to ⅛-inch thickness. Cut into same shapes as individual cakes. Repeat with second half of paste. Warm jam in small saucepan on low heat until thin. Remove top of one cake. Spread ¼ to ½ teaspoon jam on inside of each cut surface. Place one almond paste cutout on bottom layer. Top with second half of cake, jam-side down. Repeat with remaining cakes.

4. For glaze, place chocolate chips and shortening in 4-cup glass measuring cup. Microwave at MEDIUM (50% power) for 2 minutes; stir. Microwave for 2 minutes longer at MEDIUM; stir until smooth. Place 3 assembled cakes on cooling rack over bowl. Spoon chocolate glaze over each cake until top and sides are completely covered. Remove to waxed paper when glaze has stopped dripping. Repeat process until all cakes are covered. (Return chocolate glaze in bowl to glass measuring cup as needed; microwave at MEDIUM for 30 to 60 seconds to thin.)

5. Drizzle each petit four with remaining chocolate glaze. Store in single layer in airtight containers.

TIP: To make cutting the cake into shapes easier, bake the cake one day before assembling.

C H O C O L A T E   T I P

To decorate petit fours, place remaining chocolate glaze in a resealable plastic food storage bag; seal. Place the bag in a bowl of hot water for several minutes. Dry with a paper towel. Knead until the chocolate is smooth. Snip pinpoint hole in one bottom corner of the bag. Drizzle or squeeze the chocolate out of hole to decorate top of each petit four. Let stand until chocolate is set.

CHEESECAKE FILLING

1 container (8 ounces) fat free
    cream cheese

¼ cup sugar

1 egg

CHOCOLATE BATTER

1½ cups all-purpose flour

¾ cup sugar

⅓ cup unsweetened cocoa
    powder

1 teaspoon baking soda

½ teaspoon salt

1 cup water

⅓ cup Prune Purée (recipe
    follows) or prepared prune
    butter or 1 jar (2½ ounces)
    first-stage baby food prunes

1 tablespoon instant espresso
    coffee powder or
    2 tablespoons instant coffee
    granules

1 tablespoon white vinegar

2 teaspoons vanilla

½ cup semisweet chocolate chips

ALMOND TOPPING

¼ cup finely chopped blanched
    almonds

2 tablespoons sugar

BLACK BOTTOM CHEESECAKE CUPS

Makes 18 cupcakes

Preheat oven to 350°F. Line eighteen 2¾-inch (⅓-cup capacity) muffin cups with cupcake liners. Coat liners lightly with vegetable cooking spray. To make filling, in small mixer bowl, beat filling ingredients at medium speed until smooth; set aside.

To make chocolate batter, in large bowl, combine first five batter ingredients. In medium bowl, beat water, prune purée, espresso powder, vinegar and vanilla until blended. Mix into flour mixture. Spoon into muffin cups, dividing equally. Top each with heaping teaspoonful of filling. Sprinkle with chocolate chips.

To make topping, mix almonds and sugar; sprinkle over chocolate chips. Bake in center of oven about 25 minutes or until pick inserted into chocolate portion comes out clean. Cool in pans 5 minutes; remove from pans to wire racks to cool completely.

PRUNE PURÉE: Combine 1⅓ cups (8 ounces) pitted prunes and 6 tablespoons hot water in container of food processor or blender. Pulse on and off until prunes are finely chopped and smooth. Store leftovers in a covered container in the refrigerator for up to two months.

FAVORITE RECIPE FROM CALIFORNIA PRUNE BOARD

Black Bottom Cheesecake Cups

Filling (recipe follows)

3 cups all-purpose flour

2 cups sugar

⅔ cup HERSHEY'S Cocoa

2 teaspoons baking soda

1 teaspoon salt

2 cups water

⅔ cup vegetable oil

2 tablespoons white vinegar

2 teaspoons vanilla extract

FILLED RICH CHOCOLATE CUPCAKES

Makes about 2½ dozen cupcakes

Prepare Filling; set aside. Preheat oven to 350°F. Line muffin cups 2½ inches in diameter with paper bake cups. In large mixer bowl stir together flour, sugar, cocoa, baking soda and salt. Add water, oil, vinegar and vanilla; beat on medium speed 2 minutes or until well combined. Fill muffin cups ⅔ full with batter. Spoon 1 level tablespoon Filling into center of each cupcake. Bake 20 to 25 minutes or until wooden pick inserted in cake portion comes out clean. Remove to wire rack. Cool completely.

FILLING

1 package (8 ounces) cream cheese, softened

⅓ cup sugar

1 egg

⅛ teaspoon salt

1 cup HERSHEY'S Semi-Sweet Chocolate Chips or MINI CHIPS® Chocolate

In small mixer bowl combine cream cheese, sugar, egg and salt; beat until smooth and creamy. Stir in chocolate chips.

1 cup water

¾ cup egg substitute

½ cup Prune Purée (recipe follows) or prepared prune butter

2 teaspoons vanilla*

1 cup plus 2 tablespoons all-purpose flour

1 cup plus 2 tablespoons sugar

¾ cup unsweetened cocoa powder

1½ teaspoons baking powder

¼ teaspoon baking soda

¼ teaspoon salt

2 cups fat free vanilla frozen yogurt

3 ripe bananas, sliced

¾ cup prepared nonfat hot fudge chocolate sauce, warmed

*1½ tablespoons rum extract can be substituted for vanilla.

DEVIL'S FOOD CUPCAKE SPLIT

Makes 6 servings

Preheat oven to 350°F. Coat twelve 2¾-inch (⅓-cup capacity) muffin cups with vegetable cooking spray. To make cupcakes, in mixer bowl, beat water, egg substitute, prune purée and vanilla until well blended. Add flour, sugar, cocoa, baking powder, baking soda and salt; mix well. Spoon batter into prepared muffin cups, dividing equally. Bake in center of oven about 20 minutes until pick inserted into centers comes out clean. Cool in pan on wire rack 5 minutes; remove from pan to rack to cool completely. Reserve six cupcakes for another use. To serve, cut each remaining cupcake horizontally in half; place bottom half on plate. Top each with ⅓-cup scoop frozen yogurt, one sixth of banana slices, 2 tablespoons sauce and remaining cupcake half.

PRUNE PURÉE: Combine 1⅓ cups (8 ounces) pitted prunes and 6 tablespoons hot water in container of food processor or blender. Pulse on and off until prunes are finely chopped and smooth. Store leftovers in a covered container in the refrigerator for up to two months.

FAVORITE RECIPE FROM CALIFORNIA PRUNE BOARD

Sinfully Rich Cheesecakes

2 cups crushed chocolate
    cookies or vanilla wafers
    (about 8 ounces cookies)
¼ cup (½ stick) butter, melted
2½ packages (8 ounces each)
    cream cheese, softened
1 cup sugar
1½ tablespoons all-purpose flour
¼ teaspoon salt
1½ teaspoons vanilla
3 eggs
2 tablespoons whipping cream
    Caramel and Chocolate
    Toppings (recipes follow)
¾ cup chopped toasted pecans

DECADENT TURTLE CHEESECAKE

Makes one 9-inch cheesecake

Preheat oven to 450°F. For crust, combine cookie crumbs and butter; press onto bottom of 9-inch springform pan.

For filling, beat cream cheese in large bowl with electric mixer until creamy. Beat in sugar, flour, salt and vanilla; mix well. Add eggs, one at a time, beating well after each addition. Blend in cream. Pour over crust.

Bake 10 minutes; *reduce oven temperature to 200°F.* Continue baking 35 to 40 minutes or until set. Loosen cake from rim of pan; cool completely before removing rim of pan. Meanwhile, prepare Caramel and Chocolate Toppings.

Drizzle cake with toppings. Refrigerate. Sprinkle with pecans before serving.

CARAMEL TOPPING: Combine ½ (14-ounce) bag caramels and ¼ cup whipping cream in small saucepan; stir over low heat until smooth.

CHOCOLATE TOPPING: Combine 4 squares (1 ounce each) semisweet chocolate *or* 4 ounces semisweet chocolate chips, 1 teaspoon butter and 2 tablespoons whipping cream in small saucepan; stir over low heat until smooth.

Decadent Turtle Cheesecake

2 (8-ounce) packages
PHILADELPHIA BRAND®
Cream Cheese, softened
½ cup sugar
½ teaspoon vanilla
2 eggs
¾ cup prepared chocolate chip
cookie dough, divided
1 KEEBLER® READY CRUST™
Graham Cracker Pie Crust
(6-ounce or 9-inch)

CHOCOLATE CHIP COOKIE DOUGH CHEESECAKE

Makes 8 servings

1. MIX cream cheese, sugar and vanilla at medium speed with electric mixer until well blended. Add eggs; mix until blended. Drop ½ cup of the cookie dough by level teaspoonfuls into batter; fold gently.

2. POUR into crust. Dot with level teaspoonfuls of remaining ¼ cup cookie dough.

3. BAKE at 350°F, 40 minutes or until center is almost set. Cool. Refrigerate 3 hours or overnight.

COOKIES AND CREAM CHEESECAKE: Omit cookie dough. Substitute chocolate flavored pie crust for graham cracker pie crust. Stir ½ cup chopped chocolate sandwich cookies into batter. Sprinkle with additional ¼ cup chopped chocolate sandwich cookies before baking.

PREP TIME: 10 MINUTES
BAKE TIME: 40 MINUTES

Chocolate Chip Cookie Dough Cheesecake

2 cups (16 ounces) nonfat
    cottage cheese
¾ cup liquid egg substitute
⅔ cup sugar
4 ounces (½ of 8-ounce package)
    Neufchâtel cheese (light
    cream cheese), softened
⅓ cup HERSHEY'S Cocoa or
    HERSHEY'S European
    Style Cocoa
½ teaspoon vanilla extract
    Yogurt Topping (recipe
    follows)
    Sliced strawberries or
    mandarin orange segments
    (optional)

LUSCIOUS CHOCOLATE CHEESECAKE

Makes 12 servings

Heat oven to 300°F. Spray 9-inch springform pan with vegetable cooking spray. In food processor, place cottage cheese, egg substitute, sugar, Neufchâtel cheese, cocoa and vanilla; process until smooth. Pour into prepared pan.

Bake 35 minutes or until edge is set. Meanwhile, prepare Yogurt Topping. Carefully spread topping over top of warm cheesecake. Return cheesecake to oven; bake 5 minutes. With knife, loosen cheesecake from side of pan. Cool completely in pan on wire rack. Cover; refrigerate until chilled. Just before serving, remove side of pan. Serve with strawberries or oranges, if desired. Garnish as desired. Cover; refrigerate leftover cheesecake.

YOGURT TOPPING: In small bowl, stir together ⅔ cup plain nonfat yogurt and 2 tablespoons sugar until well blended.

Luscious Chocolate Cheesecake

1½ cups chocolate wafer cookie
crumbs (about 6 ounces)

4 tablespoons butter or
margarine, melted

1 envelope unflavored gelatin

1 cup milk

4 MILKY WAY® Bars
(2.15 ounces each), sliced

2 packages (8 ounces each)
cream cheese, softened

2 tablespoons granulated sugar

1 teaspoon vanilla extract

1 cup (½ pint) heavy or
whipping cream

HEAVENLY NO BAKE CHEESECAKE
Makes about 12 servings

Combine cookie crumbs and butter. Press into bottom and 2 inches up side of 8-inch springform pan; chill. Sprinkle gelatin over milk in medium saucepan. Stir over low heat until gelatin is dissolved. Add Milky Way bars and continue to stir over low heat until mixture is smooth; cool slightly. Meanwhile, beat cream cheese and sugar with electric mixer until smooth. Beat in Milky Way bar mixture and vanilla. Add cream and beat at high speed of electric mixer 4 minutes. Pour mixture into prepared crust. Chill until firm, about 4 hours. If desired, garnish with whipped cream and sliced Milky Way bars.

C H O C O L A T E   T I P

In 1911, candy bars first appeared in America. During World War I chocolate candy bars were distributed to the Army for emergency rations.

However, this all-too-delicious candy bar was too irresistible to be kept for emergency needs. The soldiers would eat them right away.

2 (8-ounce) packages
    PHILADELPHIA BRAND®
    Cream Cheese, softened
½ cup sugar
½ teaspoon vanilla
2 eggs
¾ cup mini semi-sweet chocolate
    chips, divided
1 KEEBLER® READY CRUST™
    Graham Cracker or
    Chocolate Flavored Pie
    Crust (6-ounce or 9-inch)

CHOCOLATE CHIP CHEESECAKE

Makes 8 servings

1. **MIX** cream cheese, sugar and vanilla at medium speed with electric mixer until well blended. Add eggs; mix until blended. Stir in ½ cup of the chips.

2. **POUR** into crust. Sprinkle with remaining ¼ cup chips.

3. **BAKE** at 350°F, 40 minutes or until center is almost set. Cool. Refrigerate 3 hours or overnight.

PEANUT BUTTER CHOCOLATE CHIP CHEESECAKE: Beat ⅓ cup peanut butter in with cream cheese.

BANANA CHOCOLATE CHIP CHEESECAKE: Beat ½ cup mashed ripe banana in with cream cheese.

PREP TIME: 10 MINUTES
BAKE TIME: 40 MINUTES

Chocolate Crumb Crust
(recipe follows)

3 packages (8 ounces each)
cream cheese, softened

1¼ cups sugar

½ cup dairy sour cream

¼ cup HERSHEY'S Cocoa

2 teaspoons vanilla extract

2 tablespoons all-purpose flour

3 eggs

Chocolate Leaves
(page 270)

Assorted fresh fruit, sliced
(optional)

Sweetened whipped cream or
whipped topping (optional)

CHOCOLATE FESTIVAL CHEESECAKE

Makes 10 to 12 servings

Prepare Chocolate Crumb Crust; set aside. Heat oven to 450°F. In large mixer bowl, combine cream cheese, sugar, sour cream, cocoa and vanilla; beat on medium speed until smooth. Add flour and eggs; beat well. Pour into prepared crust. Bake 10 minutes. *Without opening oven door, decrease temperature to 250°F;* continue baking 30 minutes. (Cheesecake may not appear set in middle.) *Turn off oven;* leave cheesecake in oven 30 minutes without opening door. Remove from oven. With knife, loosen cheesecake from side of pan; cool to room temperature. Refrigerate several hours or overnight; remove side of pan. Garnish with Chocolate Leaves, fruit and whipped cream, if desired. Cover; refrigerate leftovers.

CHOCOLATE CRUMB CRUST: Heat oven to 350°F. In small bowl, stir together 1¼ cups vanilla wafer crumbs (about 40 wafers), ⅓ cup powdered sugar and ⅓ cup HERSHEY'S Cocoa; stir in ¼ cup (½ stick) melted butter or margarine. Press mixture onto bottom and ½ inch up side of 9-inch springform pan. Bake 8 to 10 minutes. Cool.

Chocolate Festival Cheesecake

**Chocolate Crumb Crust
(recipe follows)**

**2 cups (12-ounce package)
HERSHEY₂S Semi-Sweet
Chocolate Chips**

**3 packages (8 ounces each)
cream cheese, softened**

**1 can (14 ounces) sweetened
condensed milk (not
evaporated milk)**

4 eggs

**¼ cup coffee-flavored liqueur
(optional)**

2 teaspoons vanilla extract

FUDGE TRUFFLE CHEESECAKE

Makes 10 to 12 servings

Heat oven to 300°F. Prepare Chocolate Crumb Crust. In microwave-safe bowl, place chocolate chips. Microwave at HIGH (100%) 1½ to 2 minutes or until chocolate is melted and smooth when stirred. In large mixer bowl, beat cream cheese until fluffy. Gradually beat in sweetened condensed milk until smooth. Add melted chocolate, eggs, liqueur, if desired and vanilla; mix well. Pour into prepared Chocolate Crumb Crust. Bake 1 hour and 5 minutes or until center is set. Remove from oven to wire rack. With knife, loosen cake from side of pan. Cool completely; remove side of pan. Refrigerate before serving. Garnish as desired. Cover; refrigerate leftovers.

CHOCOLATE CRUMB CRUST: In medium bowl, stir together 1½ cups vanilla wafer crumbs, ½ cup powdered sugar, ⅓ cup HERSHEY₂S Cocoa and ⅓ cup melted butter or margarine. Press firmly on bottom of 9-inch springform pan.

Fudge Truffle Cheesecake

2 (8-ounce) packages
PHILADELPHIA BRAND®
Cream Cheese, softened
½ cup sugar
½ teaspoon vanilla
2 eggs
4 teaspoons green crème de
menthe
1 KEEBLER® READY CRUST™
Chocolate Flavored Pie
Crust (6-ounce or 9-inch)

CRÈME DE MENTHE CHEESECAKE

Makes 8 servings

1. **MIX** cream cheese, sugar and vanilla at medium speed with electric mixer until well blended. Add eggs; mix until blended. Blend in crème de menthe. Pour into crust.

2. **BAKE** at 350°F, 40 minutes or until center is almost set. Cool. Refrigerate 3 hours or overnight. Garnish with chocolate leaves and twigs.

MINT BON BON CHEESECAKE: Substitute ¼ teaspoon peppermint extract and a few drops green food coloring for crème de menthe. Stir ½ cup mini semi-sweet chocolate chips into batter. Sprinkle with additional ¼ cup chips before baking.

PREP TIME: 10 MINUTES
BAKE TIME: 40 MINUTES

CHOCOLATE TIP

To make chocolate twigs, place 1 square semisweet chocolate in resealable plastic food storage bag. Close bag tightly and microwave on HIGH about 1 minute or until the chocolate is melted. Snip a tiny piece off one corner. Drizzle the chocolate thru snipped hole onto wax-paper lined cookie sheet in the form of a twig. Refrigerate about 30 minutes or until firm.

Crème de Menthe Cheesecake

Chocolate Crumb Crust
   (page 238)
3 packages (8 ounces each)
   cream cheese, softened
¾ cup sugar
3 eggs
⅓ cup dairy sour cream
3 tablespoons all-purpose flour
1 teaspoon vanilla extract
¼ teaspoon salt
1 cup HERSHEY'S Butterscotch
   Chips, melted*
1 cup HERSHEY'S Semi-Sweet
   Chocolate Chips, melted*
1 cup HERSHEY'S Premier
   White Chips, melted*
   Triple Drizzle (page 238,
   optional)

*To melt chips: Place chips in separate
medium microwave-safe bowls.
Microwave at HIGH (100%)
1 minute; stir. If necessary, microwave
at HIGH an additional 15 seconds at
a time, stirring after each heating, just
until chips are melted when stirred.

TRIPLE LAYER CHEESECAKE

Makes 12 to 14 servings

Heat oven to 350°F. Prepare Chocolate Crumb Crust. In large mixer bowl, beat cream cheese and sugar until smooth. Add eggs, sour cream, flour, vanilla and salt; beat until blended. Stir 1⅓ cups batter into melted butterscotch chips until smooth; pour into prepared crust. Stir 1⅓ cups batter into melted chocolate chips until smooth; pour over butterscotch layer. Stir remaining batter into melted white chips until smooth; pour over chocolate layer. Bake 55 to 60 minutes or until almost set in center. Remove from oven to wire rack. With knife, loosen cake from side of pan. Cool completely; remove side of pan. Prepare Triple Drizzle, if desired; drizzle, one flavor at a time, over top of cheesecake. Refrigerate about 3 hours. Cover; refrigerate leftover cheesecake.

continued on page 238

Triple Layer Cheesecake

Triple Layer Cheesecake continued
from page 236

CHOCOLATE CRUMB CRUST

1½ cups vanilla wafer crumbs (about 45 wafers)
½ cup powdered sugar
¼ cup HERSHEY'S Cocoa
⅓ cup butter or margarine, melted

Heat oven to 350°F. In medium bowl, stir together all ingredients. Press mixture onto bottom and 1½ inches up side of 9-inch springform pan. Bake 8 minutes. Cool completely.

TRIPLE DRIZZLE

1 tablespoon *each* HERSHEY'S Butterscotch Chips, HERSHEY'S Semi-Sweet Chocolate Chips and HERSHEY'S Premier White Chips
1½ teaspoons shortening (do not use butter, margarine or oil), divided

In small microwave-safe bowl, place butterscotch chips and ½ teaspoon shortening. Microwave at HIGH (100%) 30 seconds; stir. If necessary, microwave on HIGH an additional 15 seconds at a time, stirring after each heating, just until chips are melted when stirred. Repeat procedure with chocolate chips and white chips, using ½ teaspoon shortening for each.

2 (8-ounce) packages
   PHILADELPHIA BRAND®
   Cream Cheese, softened
½ cup sugar
½ teaspoon vanilla
2 eggs
1 cup chopped white chocolate,
   divided
1 KEEBLER® READY CRUST™
   Graham Cracker Pie Crust
   (6-ounce or 9-inch)
½ cup chopped almonds

WHITE CHOCOLATE ALMOND CHEESECAKE

Makes 8 servings

1. **MIX** cream cheese, sugar and vanilla at medium speed with electric mixer until well blended. Add eggs; mix until blended. Stir in ½ cup of the white chocolate.

2. **POUR** into crust. Sprinkle with almonds and remaining ½ cup white chocolate.

3. **BAKE** at 350°F, 40 minutes or until center is almost set. Cool. Refrigerate 3 hours or overnight.

PREP TIME: 10 MIN.
BAKE TIME: 40 MIN.

C H O C O L A T E   T I P

For the best white chocolate, always check the label to be sure cocoa butter is listed as one of the ingredients. Some products that do not contain *cocoa butter will not melt as well or have the same rich flavor as a true white chocolate.*

CRUST

½ cup (1 stick) butter
¼ cup sugar
½ teaspoon vanilla
1 cup flour

FILLING

4 (8-ounce) packages
PHILADELPHIA BRAND®
Cream Cheese, softened
½ cup sugar
1 teaspoon vanilla
4 eggs
12 ounces white chocolate,
melted, slightly cooled

WHITE CHOCOLATE CHEESECAKE

Makes 12 servings

■ Heat oven to 325°F.

CRUST

■ Cream butter, sugar and vanilla in small bowl at medium speed with electric mixer until light and fluffy. Gradually add flour, mixing at low speed until blended. Press onto bottom of 9-inch springform pan; prick with fork.

■ Bake 25 minutes or until edges are light golden brown.

FILLING

■ Beat cream cheese, sugar and vanilla at medium speed with electric mixer until well blended. Add eggs, 1 at a time, mixing at low speed after each addition, just until blended.

■ Blend in melted chocolate; pour over crust.

■ Bake 55 to 60 minutes or until center is almost set. Run knife or metal spatula around rim of pan to loosen cake; cool before removing rim of pan. Refrigerate 4 hours or overnight. Garnish with chocolate curls and powdered sugar.

MACADAMIA NUT CHEESECAKE: Stir 1 (3½-ounce) jar macadamia nuts, chopped (about ¾ cup) into batter.

PREP TIME: 35 MINUTES
BAKE TIME: 60 MINUTES

White Chocolate Cheesecake

CRUST:

> 2 cups vanilla wafer crumbs
>
> 6 tablespoons margarine or
> butter, melted

FILLING:

> 24 caramels (about 7 ounces)
>
> $\frac{1}{4}$ cup evaporated milk
>
> 1 cup toasted chopped pecans
>
> 2 packages (8 ounces each)
> PHILADELPHIA BRAND®
> Cream Cheese, softened
>
> $\frac{1}{2}$ cup sugar
>
> 1 teaspoon vanilla
>
> 2 eggs
>
> 6 squares BAKER'S® Semi-Sweet
> Chocolate, melted
>
> COOL WHIP® Whipped
> Topping, thawed (optional)
>
> Chocolate Doodles (optional)

CHOCOLATE CARAMEL PECAN CHEESECAKE

Makes 12 servings

HEAT oven to 350°F.

COMBINE crumbs and margarine in 9-inch springform pan until well mixed. Press onto bottom and 1$\frac{1}{4}$ inches up side of pan. Bake for 10 minutes.

MICROWAVE caramels and milk in large microwavable bowl on HIGH 1$\frac{1}{2}$ minutes. Stir; microwave 1 minute longer. Stir until caramels are completely melted and smooth. Pour into crust. Top with pecans.

BEAT cream cheese, sugar and vanilla until well blended. Add eggs; beat well. Mix in chocolate; pour over pecans.

BAKE for 40 minutes or until firm. Cool on wire rack. Cover; refrigerate. Garnish with whipped topping and Chocolate Doodles, if desired.

PREP TIME: 30 MINUTES

BAKE TIME: 40 MINUTES

Chocolate Caramel Pecan Cheesecake

CRUST

1 package DUNCAN HINES®
    Golden Sugar Cookie Mix
1 egg
¼ cup CRISCO® Oil or CRISCO®
    PURITAN® Canola Oil
1½ tablespoons water
½ cup finely chopped pecans *

FILLING

1¼ cups firmly packed brown
    sugar
2 tablespoons all-purpose flour
3 packages (8 ounces each)
    cream cheese, softened
3 eggs, lightly beaten
1½ teaspoons vanilla extract
1 square (1 ounce) unsweetened
    chocolate, melted
20 to 25 pecan halves (½ cup)
    Caramel flavor topping

For added flavor, toast pecans before chopping. Spread pecans in single layer on baking sheet. Toast in 350°F oven for 3 to 5 minutes or until fragrant. Cool completely.

CHOCOLATE MARBLE PRALINE CHEESECAKE

Makes 12 to 16 servings

1. Preheat oven to 350°F.

2. **For crust,** combine cookie mix, 1 egg, oil, water and chopped pecans in large bowl. Stir until thoroughly blended. Reserve 1 cup dough; set aside. Press remaining mixture into bottom of ungreased 9-inch springform pan. Bake at 350°F for 22 to 24 minutes or until edge is light brown and center is set. Remove from oven.

3. **For filling,** combine brown sugar and flour in small bowl; set aside. Place cream cheese in large bowl. Beat at low speed with electric mixer, adding brown sugar mixture gradually. Add beaten eggs and vanilla extract, mixing only until incorporated. Remove 1 cup batter to small bowl; add melted chocolate. Pour remaining plain batter onto warm crust. Drop spoonfuls of chocolate batter over plain batter. Run knife through batters to marble. Arrange pecan halves around top edge. Bake at 350°F for 45 to 55 minutes or until set. Loosen cake from sides of pan with knife or spatula. Cool completely on rack. Refrigerate 2 hours or until ready to serve.

4. To serve, remove sides of pan. Glaze top of cheesecake with caramel flavor topping. Cut into slices and serve with additional caramel flavor topping, if desired.

Chocolate Marble Praline Cheesecake

1½ cups graham cracker crumbs

1 cup sugar, divided

⅓ cup butter or margarine, melted

2 packages (8 ounces each) cream cheese, softened

2 eggs

2 tablespoons amaretto liqueur

2 teaspoons instant coffee powder

½ cup BLUE DIAMOND® Blanched Slivered Almonds, toasted

MOCHA ALMOND CHEESECAKE

Makes one 9-inch cheesecake

Preheat oven to 300°F. Combine graham cracker crumbs, ¼ cup sugar and melted butter. Press into bottom and 1½ inches up side of 9-inch springform pan. Bake 15 minutes.

In large mixing bowl, beat cream cheese and remaining ¾ cup sugar 5 minutes at medium speed of electric mixer; add eggs, one at a time, mixing well after each addition. Add liqueur and coffee powder, blending thoroughly; fold in almonds.

Pour into baked crust. Bake 40 minutes or until filling is set. Shut off oven, open door and allow cheesecake to cool in oven. When cool, remove from oven; remove rim of pan. Refrigerate to chill thoroughly before serving.

3 squares BAKER'S® Semi-Sweet
　　Chocolate
¼ cup water
1 (8-ounce) container
　　PHILADELPHIA BRAND®
　　LIGHT Pasteurized Process
　　Cream Cheese Product
½ cup light or low calorie
　　raspberry fruit spread,
　　divided
3¼ cups (8 ounces) COOL WHIP
　　LITE® Whipped Topping,
　　thawed, divided
2 tablespoons water
36 fresh raspberries
2 chocolate wafers, crushed

CHOCOLATE RASPBERRY CHEESECAKE

Makes 12 servings

MICROWAVE* chocolate with ¼ cup water in large microwavable bowl at HIGH 1 to 1½ minutes until almost melted; stir until completely melted. (Mixture will be thick.)

BEAT chocolate, cream cheese product and ¼ cup of the fruit spread. Immediately stir in 2½ cups whipped topping until smooth. Spread in 8- or 9-inch pie plate or springform pan. Freeze 3 to 4 hours.

REMOVE from freezer; let stand 15 minutes. Briefly heat and stir remaining fruit spread and 2 tablespoons water until well blended. Remove from heat. Garnish each serving with fruit spread mixture, remaining whipped topping, raspberries and cookie crumbs. Store leftover cheesecake in freezer.

*Range Top: Heat chocolate with water in saucepan over very low heat; stir constantly until just melted. Remove from heat; continue as above.

CRUST

2/3 cup all-purpose flour

1/2 cup powdered sugar

1/2 cup ground walnuts

6 tablespoons butter or
    margarine, softened

1/3 cup NESTLÉ® TOLL HOUSE®
    Baking Cocoa

FILLING

1 1/4 cups heavy whipping cream

1/4 cup granulated sugar

2 cups (12-ounce package)
    NESTLÉ® TOLL HOUSE®
    Semi-Sweet Chocolate
    Morsels

2 tablespoons seedless
    raspberry jam

Sweetened whipped cream
    (optional)

Fresh raspberries (optional)

CHOCOLATE TRUFFLE TART

Makes one 9-inch tart

FOR CRUST:

BEAT flour, powdered sugar, nuts, butter and cocoa in large mixer bowl until soft dough forms. Press dough onto bottom and side of ungreased 9- or 9½-inch fluted tart pan with removable bottom.

BAKE in preheated 350°F oven for 12 to 14 minutes or until puffed. Cool completely on wire rack.

FOR FILLING:

HEAT cream and granulated sugar in medium saucepan just until boiling, stirring occasionally. Remove from heat. Stir in morsels and jam; let stand for 5 minutes. Whisk until chocolate mixture is smooth. Transfer to small mixer bowl. Cover; chill for 45 to 60 minutes or until mixture is cool and slightly thickened.

BEAT for 20 to 30 seconds, just until color lightens slightly. Spoon into crust. Chill until firm. Remove rim of pan; garnish with whipped cream and raspberries.

Note: May be made in 9-inch pie plate following directions.

Chocolate Truffle Tart

1 envelope KNOX® Unflavored
　　Gelatine
⅓ cup cold water
2 cups (1 pint) heavy or
　　whipping cream, divided
1 package (6 ounces) semi-sweet
　　chocolate chips
1 teaspoon vanilla extract
1 cup caramels (about 22)
2 tablespoons
　　FLEISCHMANN'S®
　　Margarine
　Chocolate-Pecan Crust (recipe
　　follows)

CHOCOLATE-PECAN & CARAMEL PIE

Makes about 8 servings

In small saucepan, sprinkle unflavored gelatine over cold water; let stand 1 minute. Stir over low heat until gelatine is completely dissolved, about 3 minutes. Stir in 1 cup cream. Bring *just* to a boil, then immediately add to blender or food processor with chocolate. Process until chocolate is completely melted, about 1 minute. While processing, through feed tube, add ¾ cup cream and vanilla; process until blended. Pour into large bowl and chill until thickened, about 25 minutes.

Meanwhile, in small saucepan, combine caramels with remaining ¼ cup cream and margarine. Simmer over low heat, stirring occasionally, until caramels are completely melted and mixture is smooth. Pour into Chocolate-Pecan Crust; let stand at room temperature to cool.

With wire whisk or spoon, beat gelatine mixture until smooth. Pour over caramel mixture in prepared crust; chill until firm, about 3 hours. Garnish with additional whipped cream, pecans and chocolate curls, if desired.

CHOCOLATE-PECAN CRUST: Preheat oven to 350°F. In small bowl, combine 1 box (8½ ounces) chocolate wafer cookies, crumbled (about 2 cups crumbs), ¾ cup finely chopped pecans and ½ cup melted butter or margarine. Press onto bottom and up side of 9-inch pie plate to form high rim. Bake 10 minutes; cool.

Chocolate-Pecan & Caramel Pie

3 squares (1 ounce each)
   semisweet chocolate
¼ cup MAZOLA® Margarine
½ cup heavy cream
½ cup KARO® Light Corn Syrup
3 eggs
⅓ cup granulated sugar
⅓ cup packed brown sugar
1 jar (3½ ounces) macadamia
   nuts, coarsely chopped and
   toasted (about ¾ cup)
Easy-As-Pie Crust (recipe
   follows)
Whipped cream and
   macadamia nuts dipped in
   chocolate (optional)

CHOCOLATE MACADAMIA NUT PIE

Makes 8 servings

Preheat oven to 350°F. In small saucepan, combine chocolate and margarine; stir over low heat until melted. Remove from heat. Stir in cream and corn syrup until blended. In medium bowl, beat eggs, and sugars until mixed. Stir in chocolate mixture until blended. Stir in nuts. Pour into pie crust. Bake 40 minutes or until knife inserted in center comes out clean. Cool on wire rack. Serve with whipped cream and chocolate-dipped macadamia nuts, if desired.

PREP TIME: 20 MINUTES
BAKE TIME: 40 MINUTES, PLUS COOLING

EASY-AS-PIE CRUST
1¼ cups all-purpose flour
⅛ teaspoon salt
½ cup MAZOLA® Margarine
2 tablespoons cold water

In medium bowl, mix flour and salt. With pastry blender or 2 knives, cut in margarine until mixture resembles fine crumbs. Sprinkle water over flour mixture while tossing with fork to blend well. Press dough firmly into ball. On lightly floured surface, roll out to 12-inch circle. Fit loosely into 9-inch pie plate. Trim and flute edge.

Makes 1 (9-inch) pie crust

PREP TIME: 15 MINUTES

Chocolate Macadamia Nut Pie

Chocolate Nut Crust (recipe
follows)
¾ cup (1½ sticks) margarine or
butter
¾ cup peanut butter
½ cup firmly packed brown
sugar
5¼ cups (12 ounces) COOL
WHIP® Whipped Topping,
thawed
Peanuts (optional)
2 squares BAKER'S® Semi-Sweet
Chocolate, melted
(optional)

CHOCOLATE PEANUT BUTTER PIE

Makes 10 to 12 servings

PREPARE Chocolate Nut Crust; set aside.

BEAT margarine, peanut butter and sugar until blended.
Reserve ¼ cup whipped topping for garnish. Gently stir in
remaining 5 cups whipped topping until mixture is
smooth. Spoon into Chocolate Nut Crust.

REFRIGERATE until firm, about 4 hours. Garnish with
reserved whipped topping. Sprinkle on peanuts and drizzle
with melted chocolate, if desired.

PREP TIME: 20 MINUTES
CHILL TIME: 4 HOURS

CHOCOLATE NUT CRUST

6 squares BAKER'S® Semi-Sweet Chocolate
1 tablespoon margarine or butter
1½ cups toasted finely chopped nuts

LINE 9-inch pie plate with foil.

MICROWAVE chocolate and margarine in large
microwavable bowl on HIGH 2 minutes or until margarine
is melted. **Stir until chocolate is completely melted.**

STIR in nuts. Press mixture onto bottom and up side of
prepared pie plate. Refrigerate until firm, about 1 hour.
Remove crust from pie plate; peel off foil. Return crust to
pie plate. Refrigerate.   *Makes 1 (9-inch) crust*

PREP TIME: 15 MINUTES
CHILL TIME: 60 MINUTES

2 unbaked ready-made 9-inch
   pie crusts
6 squares BAKER'S® Semi-Sweet
   Chocolate
½ cup (1 stick) margarine or
   butter, softened
½ cup sugar
2 eggs (1 separated)
1 cup toasted ground almonds
½ cup seedless raspberry
   preserves

CHOCOLATE LINZER TART

Makes 10 servings

HEAT oven to 425°F.

FIT 1 crust into 9-inch tart pan. Bake for 5 to 8 minutes or until crust begins to brown.

MICROWAVE chocolate and 2 tablespoons of the margarine in large microwavable bowl on HIGH 2 minutes or until margarine is melted. **Stir until chocolate is completely melted.**

BEAT the remaining 6 tablespoons margarine and the sugar in large bowl until light and fluffy. Beat in 1 egg, 1 egg yolk and the almonds. Stir in melted chocolate mixture. Spread mixture evenly over crust. Top with preserves.

CUT the remaining pie crust into ½-inch strips. Arrange in lattice design over preserves. Beat the remaining egg white until foamy; brush over pastry strips.

BAKE at 425°F for 10 minutes. *Reduce heat to 350°F;* bake 30 minutes longer or until crust is golden brown. Cool on wire rack.

PREP TIME: 30 MINUTES
BAKE TIME: 40 MINUTES

CLASSIC CRISCO® SINGLE CRUST

1⅓ **cups all-purpose flour**

½ **teaspoon salt**

½ **CRISCO® Stick or ½ cup CRISCO all-vegetable shortening**

3 **tablespoons cold water**

FILLING

4 **eggs**

1 **cup sugar**

1 **cup light corn syrup**

3 **tablespoons butter or margarine, melted**

1 **teaspoon vanilla**

¼ **teaspoon salt**

2 **cups pecan halves**

½ **cup semisweet chocolate chips**

1 **tablespoon plus 1½ teaspoons bourbon, optional**

CHOCOLATE CHIP PECAN PIE

Makes 1 (9-inch) pie

1. For crust, spoon flour into measuring cup and level. Combine flour and salt in medium bowl. Cut in shortening using pastry blender (or 2 knives) until all flour is blended in to form pea-size chunks.

2. Sprinkle with water, 1 tablespoon at a time. Toss lightly with fork until dough forms a ball. Press dough between hands to form a 5- to 6-inch "pancake." Flour rolling surface and rolling pin lightly. Roll dough into circle. Trim 1 inch larger than upside-down pie plate. Loosen dough carefully. Fold dough into quarters. Unfold and press into pie plate. Fold edge under. Flute. Heat oven to 375°F.

3. For filling, beat eggs in large bowl at low speed of electric mixer until blended. Stir in sugar, corn syrup, butter, vanilla and salt with spoon until blended. Stir in nuts, chocolate chips and bourbon. Pour into unbaked pie crust.

4. Bake at 375°F for 55 to 60 minutes or until set. Cover edge with foil, if necessary, to prevent overbrowning. Cool to room temperature before serving. Refrigerate leftover pie.

Chocolate Chip Pecan Pie

CRUST

2 cups BAKER'S® ANGEL
FLAKE® Coconut

½ cup chopped pecans

½ cup (½ stick) margarine or
butter, melted

FILLING

4 squares BAKER'S® Semi-Sweet
Chocolate

2 cups KRAFT® Miniature
Marshmallows

½ cup milk

1 package (3 ounces)
PHILADELPHIA BRAND®
Cream Cheese, softened

3½ cups (8 ounces) thawed COOL
WHIP® Whipped Topping

Chocolate curls (optional)

CHOCOLATE COCONUT MARSHMALLOW PIE

Makes 1 (9-inch) pie

HEAT oven to 350°F.

MIX coconut, pecans and margarine in 9-inch pie plate; press onto bottom and up side of pie plate. Bake 20 minutes or until lightly browned. Cool.

MICROWAVE chocolate, marshmallows and milk in large microwavable bowl on HIGH 3 minutes or until marshmallows are melted. **Stir until chocolate is completely melted.**

BEAT in cream cheese until smooth. Refrigerate until slightly thickened. Gently stir in whipped topping. Spoon into crust. Refrigerate until firm, about 3 hours. Garnish with chocolate curls. Before cutting, dip bottom of pie plate briefly in hot water to loosen crust.

PREP TIME: 30 MINUTES
BAKE TIME: 20 MINUTES
CHILL TIME: 3 HOURS

Clockwise from top right: Decadent Pie (page 263), Chocolate Cream Pie (page 262) and Chocolate Coconut Marshmallow Pie

1 package (4 ounces) BAKER'S®
    GERMAN'S® Sweet
    Chocolate
⅓ cup milk
1 package (3 ounces)
    PHILADELPHIA BRAND®
    Cream Cheese, softened
2 tablespoons sugar (optional)
3½ cups (8 ounces) COOL WHIP®
    Whipped Topping, thawed
1 (9-inch) prepared crumb crust
    Chocolate shavings or curls
    (optional)

GERMAN SWEET CHOCOLATE PIE

Makes 8 servings

MICROWAVE chocolate and 2 tablespoons of the milk in large microwavable bowl on HIGH 1½ to 2 minutes or until chocolate is almost melted, stirring halfway through heating time. **Stir until chocolate is completely melted.**

BEAT in cream cheese, sugar and the remaining milk until well blended. Refrigerate to cool, about 10 minutes.

STIR in whipped topping gently until smooth. Spoon into crust. Freeze until firm, about 4 hours. Garnish with chocolate shavings or curls, if desired.

PREP TIME: 20 MINUTES
FREEZE TIME: 4 HOURS

SAUCEPAN PREPARATION: Heat chocolate and 2 tablespoons of the milk in saucepan over very low heat until chocolate is melted, stirring constantly. Remove from heat. Continue as above.

German Sweet Chocolate Pie

6 squares BAKER'S® Semi-Sweet Chocolate
½ cup corn syrup
1½ cups heavy cream
1 teaspoon vanilla
Chocolate Nut Crust (page 254)
Chocolate Shavings (optional)
Sliced strawberries (optional)

CHOCOLATE CREAM PIE
Makes 8 servings

MICROWAVE chocolate, corn syrup and ½ cup of the cream in large microwavable bowl on HIGH 2 minutes. **Stir until chocolate is completely melted.** Stir in vanilla. Cool to room temperature.

BEAT the remaining 1 cup cream until soft peaks form. Gently stir into chocolate mixture. Spoon into Chocolate Nut Crust. Refrigerate until firm, about 4 hours. Garnish with additional whipped cream, chocolate shavings and strawberries, if desired.

PREP TIME: 30 MINUTES
CHILL TIME: 4 HOURS

CHOCOLATE TIP

Chocolate shavings add a beautiful and delicious touch to your dessert. To shave chocolate, pull a vegetable peeler across the surface of 1 square semisweet chocolate. Sprinkle the shavings over your dessert.

¾ cup packed brown sugar

¾ cup corn syrup

4 squares BAKER'S® Semi-Sweet
 Chocolate

6 tablespoons margarine or
 butter

3 eggs

1⅓ cups BAKER'S® ANGEL
 FLAKE® Coconut

1 cup chopped pecans

1 unbaked (9-inch) pie shell

1¾ cups (4 ounces) thawed COOL
 WHIP® Whipped Topping

1 tablespoon bourbon
 (optional)

Chocolate shavings (optional)

DECADENT PIE

Makes 1 (9-inch) pie

HEAT oven to 350°F.

MICROWAVE brown sugar and corn syrup in large microwavable bowl on HIGH 4 minutes or until boiling. Add chocolate and margarine. **Stir until chocolate is completely melted.** Cool slightly.

ADD eggs, one at a time, beating well after each addition. Stir in coconut and pecans. Pour into pie shell.

BAKE 1 hour or until knife inserted 1 inch from center comes out clean. Cool on wire rack.

COMBINE whipped topping and bourbon; spoon or pipe onto pie. Garnish with chocolate shavings.

PREP TIME: 20 MINUTES

BAKE TIME: 1 HOUR

¼ cup cold skim milk

2 envelopes unflavored gelatin

1 cup skim milk, heated to
  boiling

⅓ cup sugar

2 tablespoons instant coffee
  granules

1 tablespoon coffee flavored
  liqueur

2 cups vanilla ice milk

1 KEEBLER® READY-CRUST™
  Chocolate Flavored pie
  crust

Reduced calorie whipped
  topping (optional)

Chocolate curls (optional)

ICED COFFEE AND CHOCOLATE PIE

Makes 8 servings

Pour ¼ cup cold milk into blender container. Sprinkle gelatin over milk and mix on low speed until blended. Let stand 3 to 4 minutes. Add hot milk; cover and process on low until gelatin dissolves, about 2 minutes. Add sugar, coffee granules, liqueur and ice milk. Cover and process until smooth. Pour into crust. Chill at least 2 hours. Garnish with whipped topping and chocolate curls, if desired.

CHOCOLATE TIP

For quick and easy chocolate curls every time, carefully pull a vegetable peeler across a 1-ounce square of semisweet chocolate. Carefully pick up each chocolate curl by inserting a wooden toothpick in the center of the curl. Place on a waxed paper-lined baking sheet. Refrigerate about 15 minutes or until firm.

Iced Coffee and Chocolate Pie

1 cup Regal Chocolate Sauce
    (page 315)
1 baked 9-inch Chocolate
    Crumb Crust (recipe
    follows)
1 quart ice cream, any flavor,
    softened

FROZEN BLACK BOTTOM PIE

Makes 8 servings

POUR ¾ cup of the Regal Chocolate Sauce into Chocolate Crumb Crust, spreading lightly to cover bottom and sides of crust. Refrigerate until set. Fill crust with ice cream. Freeze until firm, about 2 hours. Let stand at room temperature about 10 minutes before ready to serve. Top with the remaining ¼ cup Regal Chocolate Sauce.

PREP TIME: 20 MINUTES
FREEZE TIME: 2 HOURS

CHOCOLATE CRUMB CRUST

3 squares BAKER'S® Semi-Sweet Chocolate
3 tablespoons margarine or butter
1 cup graham cracker crumbs

HEAT oven to 375°F.

MICROWAVE chocolate and margarine in microwavable bowl on HIGH 2 minutes or until margarine is melted. **Stir until chocolate is completely melted.**

STIR in crumbs. Press mixture onto bottom and up sides of 9-inch tart pan or pie plate. Freeze 10 minutes. Bake for 8 minutes. Cool on wire rack.   *Makes 1 (9-inch) crust*

PREP TIME: 5 MINUTES
FREEZE TIME: 10 MINUTES
BAKE TIME: 8 MINUTES

Frozen Black Bottom Pie

1 (9-inch) HONEY MAID®
    Honey Graham Pie Crust
1 egg white, slightly beaten
¼ cup heavy cream
4 (1-ounce) squares semisweet
    chocolate
¼ cup PLANTERS® Dry Roasted
    Peanuts, coarsely chopped
1 small banana, sliced
1 (4-serving size) package
    ROYAL® Instant Vanilla
    Pudding & Pie Filling
2 cups cold milk
    Whipped topping, for garnish
    Additional coarsely chopped
    PLANTERS® Dry Roasted
    Peanuts, for garnish

BLACK BOTTOM BANANA CREAM PIE

Makes 8 servings

Preheat oven to 375°F. Brush pie crust with egg white. Bake at 375°F for 5 minutes; set aside.

In small saucepan, over low heat, heat heavy cream and chocolate until chocolate melts. Stir in peanuts. Spread evenly in pie crust. Arrange banana slices over chocolate; set aside.

Prepare pudding according to package directions for pie using cold milk; carefully pour over bananas. Chill at least 2 hours. Garnish with whipped topping and additional chopped peanuts.

Black Bottom Banana Cream Pie

1 package (4-serving size)
   vanilla cook & serve
   pudding and pie filling
   mix*
3½ cups milk
1 cup REESE'S Peanut Butter
   Chips
1 cup HERSHEY'S Semi-Sweet
   Chocolate Chips or MINI
   CHIPS®
1 baked (9-inch) pie crust

*Do not use instant pudding mix.

TWO-TONE CREAM PIE

Makes 1 (9-inch) pie

In medium saucepan, combine pudding mix and milk. Cook over medium heat, stirring constantly, until mixture comes to full boil; remove from heat. Pour 2 cups hot pudding into small bowl and add peanut butter chips; stir until chips are melted and mixture is smooth. Add chocolate chips to remaining hot pudding; stir until chips are melted and mixture is smooth. Pour chocolate mixture into baked pie crust. Gently pour and spread peanut butter mixture over top. Press plastic wrap directly onto surface. Chill several hours or overnight. Garnish as desired. Refrigerate leftovers.

C H O C O L A T E   T I P

Chocolate leaves add a beautiful touch to any dessert. Thoroughly wash and dry several lemon, rose or other non-toxic leaves. Melt ½ cup semisweet chocolate chips and 1 teaspoon vegetable shortening. With a small soft-bristled brush, brush melted chocolate onto the backs of the leaves, being careful not to drip over the edges; place on wax-paper covered tray or rack. Refrigerate until very firm. Carefully peel fresh leaves from chocolate leaves; refrigerate until ready to use.

CRUST

**1 (8-inch) Classic CRISCO®
Single Crust**

FILLING

¼ cup granulated sugar

**¼ cup firmly packed brown
sugar**

2 tablespoons all-purpose flour

⅔ cup light corn syrup

⅔ cup dark corn syrup

**¼ cup butter or margarine,
softened**

3 eggs

**1 square (1 ounce) unsweetened
chocolate, melted**

1½ teaspoons vanilla

¼ teaspoon salt

½ cup walnut pieces

¼ cup shredded coconut

**¼ cup semisweet mini chocolate
chips**

6 walnut halves

CHOCOLATE PIE

Makes 1 (8-inch) pie

1. For crust, prepare (see page 256). Do not bake. Heat oven to 450°F.

2. For filling, combine granulated sugar, brown sugar, flour, light corn syrup, dark corn syrup, butter, eggs, unsweetened chocolate, vanilla and salt in large bowl. Blend well. Fold in nut pieces, coconut and chocolate chips. Pour into unbaked pie crust. Top with nut halves.

3. Bake at 450°F 10 minutes. *Reduce oven temperature to 375°F.* Bake 40 to 45 minutes or until filling is set in center. Cover edge with foil, if necessary, to prevent overbrowning. Cool to room temperature before serving.

1¼ cups chocolate graham
    cracker crumbs
3 tablespoons sugar
¼ cup Prune Purée (recipe
    follows) or prepared prune
    butter
3 cups nonfat milk
2 packages (3.4 ounces each)
    instant chocolate pudding
    mix
1½ cups low fat nondairy
    whipped topping, divided
    Chocolate curls, for garnish
    (optional)

DOUBLE CHOCOLATE MOUSSE PIE

Makes 8 servings

Preheat oven to 375°F. Coat 9-inch pie plate with vegetable cooking spray. In large bowl, combine graham cracker crumbs and sugar. Cut in prune purée with pastry blender until mixture resembles coarse crumbs. Press evenly onto bottom and side of prepared pie plate. Bake in center of oven 15 minutes. Cool completely on wire rack.

Meanwhile, in large bowl, combine milk and pudding mixes; whisk 2 minutes. Fold in 1 cup whipped topping. Spoon into prepared crust. Chill at least 2 hours. Pipe remaining whipped topping along edge. Garnish with chocolate curls, if desired. Cut into wedges.

PRUNE PURÉE: Combine 1⅓ cups (8 ounces) pitted prunes and 6 tablespoons hot water in container of food processor or blender. Pulse on and off until prunes are finely chopped and smooth. Store leftovers in a covered container in the refrigerator for up to two months.

TIP: To make chocolate curls, draw a vegetable peeler across the surface of a room temperature square of semisweet chocolate. If curls do not form, allow chocolate square to soften slightly in a warm place for 15 to 20 minutes.

FAVORITE RECIPE FROM CALIFORNIA PRUNE BOARD

Double Chocolate Mousse Pie

CHOCOLATE AND PEAR TART

Makes 12 servings

Chocolate Tart Crust (recipe
    follows)
1 cup milk
2 egg yolks, beaten
2 tablespoons sugar
⅛ teaspoon salt
1 cup HERSHEY᾽S Semi-Sweet
    Chocolate Chips
3 large fresh pears
    Apricot Glaze (recipe follows)

Prepare Chocolate Tart Crust; set aside. In top of double
boiler over hot, not boiling, water, scald milk; gradually stir
in combined egg yolks, sugar and salt. Cook over hot water,
stirring constantly, until slightly thickened; do not boil.
Remove from heat; immediately add chocolate chips,
stirring until chips are melted and mixture is smooth. Pour
into baked tart crust. Refrigerate several hours or until
firm. Core and peel pears; cut into thin slices. Place in
circular pattern on top of filling. Immediately prepare
Apricot Glaze. Spoon over top of fruit, covering completely.
Refrigerate several hours or until firm; remove side of pan.
Serve cold. Cover; refrigerate leftovers.

CHOCOLATE TART CRUST: Heat oven to 325°F. Grease and
flour 9-inch round tart pan with removable bottom. In
small mixer bowl, stir together ¾ cup all-purpose flour,
¼ cup powdered sugar and 1 tablespoon HERSHEY᾽S
Cocoa. At low speed of electric mixer, blend in
6 tablespoons chilled margarine until smooth. Press evenly
with fingers onto bottom and up side of prepared pan.
Bake 10 to 15 minutes; cool.

continued on page 276

Chocolate and Pear Tart

Chocolate and Pear Tart, continued
from page 274

APRICOT GLAZE

¾ **teaspoon unflavored gelatin**

 2 **teaspoons cold water**

½ **cup apricot nectar**

¼ **cup sugar**

 1 **tablespoon arrowroot**

 1 **teaspoon lemon juice**

In small cup, sprinkle gelatin over cold water; let stand several minutes to soften. In small saucepan, combine apricot nectar, sugar, arrowroot and lemon juice; cook over medium heat, stirring constantly, until mixture is thickened. Remove from heat; immediately add gelatin mixture. Stir until smooth.

1 tub (8 ounces) COOL WHIP®
  Whipped Topping, thawed
1 prepared graham cracker
  crumb crust (6 ounces)
1 cup cold milk
1 package (4-serving size)
  JELL-O® Chocolate Flavor
  Instant Pudding & Pie
  Filling
1 cup cherry pie filling

BLACK FOREST PIE

Makes 8 servings

SPREAD 1 cup of the whipped topping onto bottom of crust.

POUR milk into medium bowl. Add pudding mix. Beat with wire whisk 2 minutes. Gently stir in 1½ cups of the whipped topping. Spread pudding mixture over whipped topping in crust.

SPREAD remaining whipped topping over pudding mixture, leaving a 1-inch border and forming a slight depression in center of whipped topping. Spoon cherry pie filling into center.

REFRIGERATE 2 hours or until set.

Black Forest Pie

1 package (6 squares) BAKER'S®
   Premium White Chocolate,
   divided
¼ cup milk
½ cup sour cream
1 tub (8 ounces) COOL WHIP®
   Whipped Topping, thawed
1 prepared graham cracker
   crumb crust (6 ounces)
1 cup cherry pie filling

WHITE CHOCOLATE CHERRY SATIN PIE

Makes 8 servings

MICROWAVE 5½ squares of the white chocolate and milk in medium microwavable bowl on HIGH 2 minutes or until chocolate is almost melted, stirring halfway through heating time. **Stir until chocolate is completely melted.** Cool 15 minutes or until room temperature.

STIR sour cream and whipped topping into chocolate mixture with wire whisk until smooth. Spoon mixture into crust.

REFRIGERATE 2 hours. Just before serving, top with pie filling. Place remaining ½ square white chocolate in small heavy-duty zipper-style plastic bag. Flatten bag and close tightly. Microwave on HIGH about 30 seconds or until chocolate is almost melted. Gently squeeze closed bag until chocolate is completely melted. Press chocolate into 1 corner of bag; twist bag to tightly contain chocolate in corner. Holding twisted bag tightly, snip a tiny piece (about ⅛ inch) off 1 corner of bag. Holding twisted bag tightly, gently squeeze bag to drizzle white chocolate through opening over pie.

1 cup sugar

⅓ cup cocoa

¼ cup cornstarch

2½ tablespoons all-purpose flour

¼ teaspoon salt

2½ cups milk

2 egg yolks, slightly beaten

2 tablespoons margarine

1 teaspoon vanilla extract

3 firm, medium DOLE®
   Bananas, peeled

Crumb-Nut Crust (recipe
   follows)

Frozen whipped topping,
   thawed

DOLE® Chopped Almonds or
   peanuts

Maraschino cherries

CHOCOLATE BANANA SPLIT PIE

Makes 8 servings

■ **MICROWAVE DIRECTIONS:** In 2-quart microwave bowl, combine sugar, cocoa, cornstarch, flour and salt. Blend in milk and egg yolks. Microwave on HIGH (100% power) 6 to 8 minutes, whisking every 2 minutes or until mixture begins to boil. Microwave additional minute until thickened. Blend in margarine and vanilla. Press plastic wrap onto surface; cool.

■ Slice 2 bananas; arrange over bottom of crust. Pour filling over bananas; press plastic wrap onto filling. Refrigerate 4 to 5 hours.

■ Remove plastic wrap. Top pie with dollops of whipped topping. Slice remaining banana. Garnish with almonds, remaining sliced banana and cherries.

CRUMB-NUT CRUST

6 tablespoons margarine

1¼ cups graham cracker crumbs

¼ cup DOLE® Chopped Almonds

In small microwavable bowl, microwave margarine 45 seconds or until melted. Stir in graham cracker crumbs and almonds.

Press on bottom and up side of greased microwavable 9-inch pie plate. Microwave 1½ to 2 minutes. Cool.

Makes 1 (9-inch) pie crust

1 package (4-serving size)
   JELL-O® Vanilla Flavor
   Pudding & Pie Filling
1¾ cups half and half or milk
1 Chocolate Crumb Crust
   (page 266), baked in
   9-inch tart pan and cooled
1 pint raspberries
2 squares BAKER'S® Semi-Sweet
   Chocolate, melted

CHOCOLATE RASPBERRY TART

Makes 8 to 10 servings

MICROWAVE pie filling mix and half and half in large microwavable bowl on HIGH 3 minutes; stir well. Microwave 3 minutes longer; stir again. Microwave 1 minute or until mixture comes to a boil. Cover surface with plastic wrap. Refrigerate at least 4 hours.

SPOON filling into Chocolate Crumb Crust just before serving. Arrange raspberries on top of filling. Drizzle with melted chocolate.

PREP TIME: 30 MINUTES

CHILL TIME: 4 HOURS

SAUCEPAN PREPARATION: Combine pie filling mix and half and half in 2-quart saucepan. Cook over medium heat until mixture comes to a full boil, stirring constantly. Continue as above.

Chocolate Raspberry Tart

3 eggs

1 cup milk

½ cup buttermilk baking mix

½ cup KARO® Light or Dark Corn Syrup

¼ cup MAZOLA® Margarine, softened

1 cup (6 ounces) semisweet chocolate chips, melted

1 can (21 ounces) cherry pie filling

¼ teaspoon almond extract

1 cup heavy cream, whipped

Chocolate curls (optional)

JUBILEE PIE

Makes 1 (9-inch) pie

Preheat oven to 350°F. Grease 9-inch pie plate. In food processor or blender, beat eggs, milk, baking mix, corn syrup, margarine and melted chocolate 1 minute. Pour into prepared pie plate; let stand 5 minutes. Bake 35 to 40 minutes or until filling is puffed and set. Cool on wire rack 1 hour; center will fall, forming well. While pie bakes, mix cherry pie filling and almond extract; refrigerate. Fill center of cooled pie with cherry mixture. Refrigerate at least 1 hour. Before serving, pipe or swirl whipped cream around edge. Garnish with chocolate curls.

PREP TIME: 20 MINUTES

BAKE TIME: 40 MINUTES, PLUS COOLING AND CHILLING

C H O C O L A T E   T I P

For perfect chocolate curls every time, melt 2 ounces of chocolate and 1 teaspoon shortening until smooth. Pour melted chocolate onto back of baking pan. Spread ¼ inch thick with metal spatula. Let stand in cool, dry place until firm. (Do not refrigerate.) When chocolate is firm, use small metal pancake turner to form curls. Hold pancake turner at a 45° angle and push under the chocolate so it forms a curl on top of the pancake turner. Using a toothpick, transfer the curls to waxed paper. Store in a cool dry place until ready to use.

Jubilee Pie

1 package (4¾ ounces) vanilla
    pudding and pie filling mix
3½ cups milk
1 cup REESE'S Peanut Butter
    Chips
1 cup HERSHEY'S Semi-Sweet
    Chocolate Chips or Semi-
    Sweet Chocolate Chunks
Whipped topping (optional)

TWO GREAT TASTES PUDDING PARFAITS

Makes about 4 to 6 servings

In large heavy saucepan, combine pudding mix and 3½ cups milk (rather than amount listed in package directions). Cook over medium heat, stirring constantly, until mixture comes to full boil. Remove from heat; divide hot mixture between 2 heatproof medium bowls. Immediately stir peanut butter chips into mixture in one bowl and chocolate chips into mixture in second bowl. Stir both mixtures until chips are melted and mixture is smooth. Cool slightly, stirring occasionally.

In parfait glasses, wine glasses or dessert dishes, alternately layer peanut butter and chocolate mixtures. Place plastic wrap directly onto surface of each dessert; refrigerate several hours or overnight. Garnish with whipped topping, if desired.

Two Great Tastes Pudding Parfaits

6 to 6½ ounces Mexican
　　chocolate, coarsely
　　chopped*
1½ cups heavy or whipping
　　cream, divided
3 tablespoons golden rum
　　(optional)
¾ teaspoon vanilla
　　Additional whipped cream for
　　garnish
　　Sliced almonds for garnish
　　Cookies (optional)

*Or, substitute 6 ounces semisweet
chocolate, coarsely chopped,
1 tablespoon ground cinnamon and
¼ teaspoon almond extract for
Mexican chocolate.

CHOCOLATE–RUM PARFAITS

Makes 4 servings

Combine chocolate and 3 tablespoons cream in top of double boiler. Heat over simmering water until smooth, stirring occasionally. Gradually stir in rum, if desired; remove top pan from heat. Let stand at room temperature 15 minutes to cool slightly.

Combine remaining cream and vanilla in small chilled bowl. Beat with electric mixer at low speed, then gradually increase speed until stiff, but not dry, peaks form.

Gently fold whipped cream into cooled chocolate mixture until uniform in color. Spoon mousse into 4 individual dessert dishes. Refrigerate 2 to 3 hours until firm. Garnish with additional whipped cream and sliced almonds. Serve with cookies, if desired.

Chocolate-Rum Parfaits

14 chocolate sandwich cookies,
   crushed (1 cup)
1 tub (8 ounces) COOL WHIP®
   Whipped Topping, thawed

CHOCOLATE COOKIE PARFAITS

Makes 4 servings

LAYER crushed cookies alternately with whipped topping in 4 (6-ounce) dessert glasses, ending with whipped topping.

REFRIGERATE until ready to serve.

TURTLE CHOCOLATE COOKIE PARFAITS: Prepare parfaits as directed above except add layers of caramel sauce or dessert topping, and chopped pecans between layers of crushed cookies and whipped topping.

2 cups cold skim milk, divided
4 ounces Neufchâtel Cheese
1 package (4-serving size)
   JELL-O® Chocolate Flavor
   Fat Free Sugar Free Instant
   Reduced Calorie Pudding
   & Pie Filling
1 package (15 ounces)
   ENTENMANN'S® Fat Free
   Chocolate Loaf, cubed
1 can (20 ounces) reduced-
   calorie cherry pie filling
1 square BAKER'S® Semi-Sweet
   Chocolate, grated

BLACK FOREST PARFAITS

Makes 12 servings

In blender container, process ½ cup of the milk and cheese until smooth. Add remaining 1½ cups milk and pudding mix; blend until smooth. Divide cake cubes evenly among 12 dessert dishes. Spoon cherry pie filling over cake cubes, reserving a few cherries for garnish. Top with pudding mixture. Refrigerate until ready to serve. Garnish with reserved cherries and chocolate.

2 cups cold milk

1 package (4-serving size)
   JELL-O® Chocolate Flavor
   Instant Pudding & Pie
   Filling

14 chocolate sandwich cookies,
   finely crushed (about
   1½ cups)

2 cups thawed COOL WHIP®
   Whipped Topping

MUD SLIDES

Makes 4 servings

LINE bottoms and sides of 2 loaf pans with wet paper towels. Tilt 2 (12-ounce) glasses in each pan.

POUR milk into 1-quart container with tight-fitting lid. Add pudding mix; cover tightly. Shake vigorously at least 45 seconds; pour evenly into glasses.

GENTLY stir 1¼ cups of the cookies into whipped topping with wire whisk in medium bowl until blended. Spoon evenly over pudding in glasses; sprinkle with remaining ¼ cup cookies.

REFRIGERATE until ready to serve.

COOL TIPS: Other pudding slide combinations are vanilla pudding with peanut butter cookies or pistachio pudding with oatmeal cookies.

1 envelope unflavored gelatin

1½ cups skim milk

3 tablespoons sugar

2 cups cooked rice

2 cups frozen light whipped
   topping, thawed

1 tablespoon almond-flavored
   liqueur

½ teaspoon vanilla extract
   Vegetable cooking spray
   Bittersweet Chocolate Sauce
   (recipe follows)

2 tablespoons sliced almonds,
   toasted

BAVARIAN RICE CLOUD WITH BITTERSWEET CHOCOLATE SAUCE

Makes 10 servings

Sprinkle gelatin over milk in small saucepan; let stand
1 minute or until gelatin is softened. Cook over low heat,
stirring constantly, until gelatin dissolves. Add sugar; stir
until it dissolves. Add rice; stir until well blended. Cover
and chill until the consistency of unbeaten egg whites. Fold
in whipped topping, liqueur and vanilla. Spoon into 4-cup
mold coated with cooking spray. Cover and chill until firm.
To serve, unmold onto serving platter. Spoon Bittersweet
Chocolate Sauce over rice dessert. Sprinkle with toasted
almonds.

BITTERSWEET CHOCOLATE SAUCE

3 tablespoons unsweetened cocoa

3 tablespoons sugar

½ cup low-fat buttermilk

1 tablespoon almond-flavored liqueur

Combine cocoa and sugar in small saucepan. Add
buttermilk, mixing well. Cook over medium heat until
sugar dissolves. Stir in liqueur; remove from heat.

TIP: Unmold gelatin desserts onto slightly dampened plate.
This will allow you to move the mold and position it where
you want it on the plate.

FAVORITE RECIPE FROM **USA RICE COUNCIL**

*Bavarian Rice Cloud with
Bittersweet Chocolate Sauce*

1 envelope unflavored gelatin

¼ cup cold water

2 tablespoons reduced-calorie tub margarine

1½ cups cold skim milk, divided

½ cup sugar

⅓ cup HERSHEY'S Cocoa or HERSHEY'S European Style Cocoa

2½ teaspoons vanilla extract, divided

1 envelope (1.3 ounces) dry whipped topping mix

LUSCIOUS COLD CHOCOLATE SOUFFLÉS

Makes 6 servings

Measure lengths of foil to fit around 6 small soufflé dishes (about 4 ounces each); fold in thirds lengthwise. Tape securely to outside of dishes to form collar, allowing collar to extend 1 inch above rims of dishes. Lightly oil inside of foil.

In small microwave-safe bowl, sprinkle gelatin over water; let stand 2 minutes to soften. Microwave at HIGH (100%) 40 seconds; stir thoroughly. Stir in margarine until melted; let stand 2 minutes or until gelatin is completely dissolved. In small mixer bowl, stir together 1 cup milk, sugar, cocoa and 2 teaspoons vanilla. Beat on low speed of electric mixer while gradually pouring in gelatin mixture. Beat until well blended. Prepare topping mix as directed on package, using remaining ½ cup milk and remaining ½ teaspoon vanilla; carefully fold into chocolate mixture until well blended.

Spoon into prepared soufflé dishes, filling ½-inch from top of collars. Cover; refrigerate until firm, about 3 hours. Carefully remove foil. Garnish as desired.

Note: Six (6-ounce) custard cups may be used in place of soufflé dishes; omit foil collar.

Luscious Cold Chocolate Soufflés

1 package (8 ounces) BAKER'S®
Semi-Sweet Chocolate

⅔ cup corn syrup

4 eggs

¼ cup milk

1 package (3 ounces)
PHILADELPHIA BRAND®
Cream Cheese, cubed and
softened

Powdered sugar (optional)

CHOCOLATE PUFF

Makes 6 servings

HEAT oven to 375°F.

MICROWAVE chocolate and corn syrup in large microwavable bowl on HIGH 2 minutes. **Stir until chocolate is completely melted.** Cool slightly.

BLEND eggs and milk in blender or food processor until smooth. With blender running, gradually add cream cheese, blending until smooth. Add chocolate mixture; blend until well mixed. Pour into ungreased 1½-quart soufflé or baking dish.

BAKE for 50 to 55 minutes or until knife inserted into center comes out clean. Sprinkle with powdered sugar, if desired.

PREP TIME: 15 MINUTES

BAKE TIME: 50 TO 55 MINUTES

SAUCEPAN PREPARATION: Heat chocolate and corn syrup in heavy 2-quart saucepan over very low heat until chocolate is melted, stirring constantly. Continue as above.

From top to bottom: Chocolate Puff and Easy Chocolate Mousse (page 296)

18 large KRAFT® Jet Puffed
   Marshmallows
¼ cup milk
 2 squares BAKER'S®
   Unsweetened Chocolate,
   chopped
 1 cup heavy cream
¼ cup sugar
   Fresh raspberries (optional)
   Chocolate Doodles (optional)

EASY CHOCOLATE MOUSSE

Makes 4 to 6 servings

MICROWAVE marshmallows and milk in large microwavable bowl on HIGH 1½ minutes. Stir until smooth. Add chocolate; stir until melted.

BEAT cream and sugar in separate bowl until stiff peaks form. Gently stir into chocolate mixture. Pour into individual dessert dishes. Refrigerate 2 hours. Garnish with raspberries and Chocolate Doodles (see Chocolate Tip), if desired.

PREP TIME: 15 MINUTES

CHILL TIME: 2 HOURS

SAUCEPAN PREPARATION: Heat marshmallows and milk in medium saucepan over low heat until marshmallows are melted, stirring constantly. Continue as above.

C H O C O L A T E   T I P

To make chocolate doodles, melt 1(1- ounce) square of semisweet chocolate in a resealable plastic food storage bag. Snip a tiny piece off one corner of the bag. Drizzle the chocolate into free-form designs onto waxed paper-lined cookie sheets. Or, draw a design on paper, cover with waxed paper and drizzle the chocolate over the design. Refrigerate about 30 minutes or until firm. Carefully pull waxed paper from chocolate doodle.

1 package ladyfingers (24)

½ cup KAHLÚA®, divided

6 eggs, separated

8 ounces semi-sweet chocolate,
     melted and cooled

½ cup sugar

KAHLÚA® CREAM

½ cup heavy or whipping cream

1 tablespoon sugar

1 tablespoon KAHLÚA®

CHOCOLATE KAHLÚA® EUPHORIA

Makes 8 servings

Separate ladyfingers on paper towels; sprinkle with ¼ cup Kahlúa®. Butter 1½-quart soufflé dish fitted with 2-inch foil collar (or use 8 individual dessert dishes or wine goblets). Arrange ladyfingers around bottom and sides of soufflé dish (or place 3 ladyfingers in the bottom of each dessert dish).

Beat egg yolks lightly in large bowl. Stir 2 tablespoons cooled, melted chocolate into yolks, then stir in remaining chocolate. Beat egg whites to soft peaks with electric mixer on high speed in another large bowl; gradually beat in ½ cup sugar until stiff peaks form. Beat in ¼ cup Kahlúa®.

Fold egg white mixture into chocolate mixture until no streaks of white remain. Spoon mixture into soufflé dish (or divide among dessert dishes). Cover; chill several hours or until firm.

For Kahlúa® Cream, beat cream until thickened; beat in 1 tablespoon sugar and 1 tablespoon Kahlúa®. Serve Kahlúa® Cream with dessert or pipe on top.

FRUIT IN A CHOCOLATE CLOUD

Makes 12 servings

Yogurt Cheese (recipe follows)

2 cups (1 pint) fresh strawberries, rinsed and drained

¼ cup sugar

¼ cup HERSHEY'S Cocoa or HERSHEY'S European Style Cocoa

2 tablespoons hot water

2 teaspoons vanilla extract, divided

½ to 1 teaspoon freshly grated orange peel (optional)

2 envelopes (1.3 ounces each) dry whipped topping mix

1 cup cold skim milk

2 large bananas, sliced

Prepare Yogurt Cheese. Remove hulls of strawberries; cut strawberries in half vertically. In medium bowl, stir together sugar, cocoa and water until smooth and well blended. Stir in 1 teaspoon vanilla. Gradually stir in Yogurt Cheese and orange peel, if desired; blend thoroughly. In large mixer bowl, prepare topping mixes as directed on packages, using 1 cup milk and remaining 1 teaspoon vanilla; fold into chocolate mixture.

Into 1½-quart glass serving bowl, carefully spoon half of chocolate mixture; place one-half of strawberry halves, cut sides out, around inside of entire bowl. Layer banana slices over chocolate mixture. Cut remaining strawberry halves into smaller pieces; layer over banana slices. Carefully spread remaining chocolate mixture over fruit. Cover; refrigerate several hours before serving. Garnish as desired.

YOGURT CHEESE: Use two 8-ounce containers vanilla lowfat yogurt, no gelatin added. Line non-rusting colander or sieve with large piece of double thickness cheesecloth or large coffee filter; place colander over deep bowl. Spoon yogurt into prepared colander; cover with plastic wrap. Refrigerate until liquid no longer drains from yogurt, about 24 hours. Remove yogurt from cheesecloth and place in separate bowl; discard liquid.

Fruit in a Chocolate Cloud

⅓ cup sugar

¼ cup HERSHEY'S Cocoa

3 tablespoons cornstarch

2⅔ cups lowfat 2% milk

1 teaspoon vanilla extract

Peach Sauce (recipe follows)

⅓ cup frozen light non-dairy whipped topping, thawed

CREAMY CHOCOLATE AND PEACH LAYERED PUDDING

Makes 6 servings

In medium saucepan, stir together sugar, cocoa and cornstarch; gradually stir in milk. Cook over medium heat, stirring constantly, until mixture comes to a boil; boil 1 minute. Remove from heat; stir in vanilla. Press plastic wrap directly onto surface. Cool completely.

Meanwhile, prepare Peach Sauce. In 6 individual dessert dishes, layer chocolate mixture and Peach Sauce. Cover; refrigerate until cold. Serve with dollop of whipped topping. Garnish as desired.

PEACH SAUCE: In blender container, place 1½ cups fresh peach slices and 1 tablespoon sugar. Cover; blend until smooth. In medium microwave-safe bowl, stir together ¼ cup water and 1½ teaspoons cornstarch until smooth. Add peach mixture; stir. Microwave at HIGH (100%) 2½ to 3 minutes or until mixture boils, stirring after each minute. Cool completely.

Creamy Chocolate and Peach Layered Pudding

1 package Duncan Hines® Moist Deluxe Devil's Food Cake Mix

1 can (14 ounces) sweetened condensed milk

1 cup cold water

1 package (4-serving size) vanilla instant pudding and pie filling mix

2 cups whipping cream, whipped

2 tablespoons orange juice, divided

2½ cups sliced fresh strawberries, divided

1 pint fresh raspberries, divided

2 kiwifruit, peeled and sliced, divided

1½ cups frozen whipped topping, thawed, for garnish

Mint leaves, for garnish (optional)

TRIFLE SPECTACULAR

Makes 10 to 12 servings

1. Preheat oven to 350°F. Grease and flour two 9-inch round cake pans.

2. Prepare, bake and cool cake following package directions for original recipe. Cut one cake layer into 1-inch cubes. Freeze other cake layer for later use.

3. Combine sweetened condensed milk and water in large bowl. Stir until blended. Add pudding mix. Beat until thoroughly blended. Chill 5 minutes. Fold whipped cream into pudding mixture.

4. To assemble, spread 2 cups pudding mixture into 3-quart trifle dish (or 3-quart clear glass bowl with straight sides). Arrange half the cake cubes over pudding mixture. Sprinkle with 1 tablespoon orange juice. Layer with 1 cup strawberry slices, half the raspberries and one-third of kiwifruit slices. Repeat layers. Top with remaining pudding mixture. Garnish with whipped topping, remaining ½ cup strawberry slices, kiwifruit slices and mint leaves, if desired.

TIP: Since the different layers contribute to the beauty of this recipe, arrange the fruit pieces to show attractively along the sides of the trifle dish.

Trifle Spectacular

1 (12 ounce) package BAKER'S® Semi-Sweet Real Chocolate Chips

1 tablespoon shortening

1 envelope unflavored gelatin

½ cup cold water

1 (8 ounce) container Light PHILADELPHIA BRAND® Pasteurized Process Cream Cheese Product

¼ cup sugar or 6 packets sugar substitute

½ cup orange juice

1 teaspoon grated orange peel

2 cups thawed COOL WHIP® Whipped Topping

ORANGE PEARLS IN CHOCOLATE SHELLS

Makes 12 servings

■ Cover outside of twelve seashells with foil, smoothing until tight.

■ Melt chocolate chips with shortening in small saucepan over low heat, stirring until smooth.

■ Spread chocolate mixture thinly over each foil-covered seashell with brush or small rubber spatula. Chill 10 minutes, keeping remaining chocolate mixture warm. Apply second coat of chocolate mixture. Chill until set.

■ Remove chocolate-covered foil from seashell; carefully peel foil from chocolate. Cover chocolate shell; chill until ready to serve.

■ Soften gelatin in water in small saucepan; stir over low heat until dissolved.

■ Beat cream cheese product and sugar in large mixing bowl at medium speed with electric mixer until well blended. Stir in gelatin, orange juice and peel. Chill until thickened but not set.

▨ Beat cream cheese mixture until light and fluffy; fold in whipped topping.

▨ Spoon approximately ⅓ cup cream cheese mixture into each chocolate shell. Garnish with chocolate lace, (see Chocolate Tip) orange segments and fresh mint leaf, if desired.

Variation: Substitute twelve paper-lined muffin cups for seashells.

TIP: If chocolate shell cracks, brush crack with melted chocolate. Refrigerate until firm.

PREP TIME: 1 HOUR PLUS CHILLING

C H O C O L A T E   T I P

To make a chocolate lace garnish, melt two (1-ounce) squares of Baker's® Semi-Sweet chocolate with 1½ teaspoons shortening. Cool slightly. Poor chocolate mixture into a small squeeze bottle or pastry tube fitted with a small writing tip. Pipe a design onto waxed paper-lined cookie sheets. Refrigerate until chocolate is set. Carefully peel waxed paper from chocolate design.

3 egg whites

⅛ teaspoon cream of tartar

¾ cup sugar

1 teaspoon vanilla extract

2 tablespoons HERSHEY'S Cocoa

1¾ cups (10-ounce package) HERSHEY'S Semi-Sweet Chocolate Chunks or 2 cups (12-ounce package) HERSHEY'S Semi-Sweet Chocolate Chips

CHOCOLATE CLOUDS

Makes 30 cookies

Preheat oven to 300°F. Cover cookie sheet with parchment paper or foil. In large bowl, beat egg whites and cream of tartar at high speed of electric mixer until soft peaks form. Gradually add sugar and vanilla, beating well after each addition until stiff peaks hold, sugar is dissolved and mixture is glossy. Sift cocoa onto egg white mixture; gently fold just until combined. Fold in chocolate chunks. Drop by heaping tablespoonfuls onto prepared cookie sheet. Bake 35 to 45 minutes or just until dry. Cool slightly; peel paper from cookies. Store, covered, at room temperature.

Chocolate Clouds

1 envelope (1.3 ounces) dry
   whipped topping mix
1 tablespoon HERSHEY'S
   Cocoa
½ cup cold skim milk
½ teaspoon vanilla extract
   Assorted fresh fruit, cut up
   Chocolate Sauce (recipe
   follows)

FRUIT–FILLED CHOCOLATE DREAMS

Makes 5 servings

Place foil on cookie sheet. In small mixer bowl, stir together topping mix and cocoa. Add ½ cup milk and ½ teaspoon vanilla. Beat on high speed of electric mixer until stiff peaks form. Spoon topping into 5 mounds onto prepared cookie sheet. With spoon, shape into 4-inch shells. Freeze until firm, about 1 hour. To serve, fill center of each frozen shell with about ⅓ cup assorted fresh fruit; drizzle with 1 tablespoon Chocolate Sauce. Garnish as desired. Serve immediately.

CHOCOLATE SAUCE

¾ cup sugar
⅓ cup HERSHEY'S Cocoa
1 tablespoon cornstarch
¾ cup water
1 tablespoon margarine
1 teaspoon vanilla extract

In small saucepan, combine sugar, cocoa and cornstarch; gradually stir in water. Cook over medium heat, stirring constantly, until mixture comes to a boil; boil 1 minute. Remove from heat; add margarine and vanilla, stirring until smooth. Cover; refrigerate until cold.

Fruit-Filled Chocolate Dreams

⅓ cup unsweetened cocoa
    powder

2 tablespoons all-purpose flour

1 square (1 ounce) semisweet
    chocolate, finely chopped

3 egg whites

¼ teaspoon cream of tartar

¼ teaspoon salt

2 cups powdered sugar

FUDGE MERINGUES

Makes 2 dozen cookies

1. Preheat oven to 300°F. Combine cocoa, flour and chocolate in small bowl; set aside. Beat egg whites in medium bowl with electric mixer at high speed until foamy. Add cream of tartar and salt; beat until soft peaks form. Gradually beat in powdered sugar; beat until stiff peaks form. Fold in chocolate mixture.

2. Drop mixture by rounded tablespoonfuls onto cookie sheets lined with parchment paper. Bake 20 minutes or until cookies are crisp when lightly touched with fingertip (cookies will crack). Slide parchment paper onto wire racks; cool completely. Carefully remove cookies from parchment paper. Cookies are best when eaten the day they are baked but can be stored in an airtight container for up to 2 days. Cookies will become crispier when stored.

Fudge Meringues

2 egg whites
¼ teaspoon cream of tartar
Dash salt
¾ cup sugar
¼ teaspoon vanilla extract
Chocolate Filling (recipe
follows)
1 package (10 ounces) frozen
strawberries in syrup,
thawed

CHOCOLATE–FILLED MERINGUE SHELLS WITH STRAWBERRY SAUCE

Makes 10 servings

Heat oven to 275°F. Line 10 muffin cups (2½ inches in diameter) with paper bake cups. In small mixer bowl, beat egg whites with cream of tartar and salt at high speed of electric mixer until soft peaks form. Beat in sugar, 1 tablespoon at a time, beating well after each addition until stiff peaks hold their shape, sugar is dissolved and mixture is glossy. Fold in vanilla. Spoon about 3 tablespoons mixture in each muffin cup. Push mixture up sides of muffin cups forming well in center.

Bake 1 hour or until meringues turn delicate cream color and feel dry to the touch. Cool in pan on wire rack. Before serving, carefully remove paper from shells. For each serving, spoon 1 heaping tablespoonful Chocolate Filling into meringue shell. In blender container, place strawberries with syrup. Cover; blend until smooth. Spoon over filled shells. Garnish as desired. Peel paper bake cups from remaining shells; store shells loosely covered at room temperature.

CHOCOLATE FILLING: In small mixer bowl, beat 4 ounces (½ of 8-ounce package) softened Neufchâtel cheese (light cream cheese) and ¼ cup HERSHEY₂S Cocoa on medium speed of electric mixer until blended. Gradually add ¾ cup powdered sugar, beating until well blended. Fold in 1 cup frozen light non-dairy whipped topping, thawed.

Chocolate-Filled Meringue Shells with Strawberry Sauce

4 squares BAKER'S®
   Unsweetened Chocolate
2 tablespoons margarine or
   butter
4 cups powdered sugar
½ cup milk
1 teaspoon vanilla

EASY FUDGE FROSTING

*Makes about 2½ cups or enough to frost tops and sides
of 2 (8- to 9-inch) layer cakes*

MICROWAVE chocolate and margarine in large
microwavable bowl on HIGH 1 minute or until margarine
is melted. **Stir until chocolate is completely melted.**

STIR in sugar, milk and vanilla until smooth. Let stand, if
necessary, until of spreading consistency, stirring
occasionally. Spread quickly. (Add 2 to 3 teaspoons
additional milk if frosting becomes too thick.)

PREP TIME: 10 MINUTES

---

6 squares BAKER'S® Semi-Sweet
   Chocolate
¼ cup (½ stick) margarine or
   butter
½ cup chopped nuts

FUDGE NUT SAUCE

Makes ⅔ cup

MICROWAVE chocolate and margarine in large
microwavable bowl on HIGH 2 minutes or until margarine
is melted. **Stir until chocolate is completely melted.** Stir in
nuts. (If sauce begins to harden, reheat 30 seconds to
1 minute in microwave.) Serve over ice cream or cake.

PREP TIME: 10 MINUTES

2 squares BAKER'S®
    Unsweetened Chocolate
⅓ cup water
½ cup sugar
3 tablespoons margarine or
    butter
¼ teaspoon vanilla

REGAL CHOCOLATE SAUCE

Makes about 1 cup

MICROWAVE chocolate and water in microwavable bowl on HIGH 1½ minutes. **Stir until chocolate is completely melted.**

STIR in sugar. Microwave 1 minute. Stir. Microwave 2 minutes longer; stir in margarine and vanilla.

PREP TIME: 10 MINUTES

SAUCEPAN PREPARATION: Heat chocolate and water in saucepan over low heat, stirring constantly, until chocolate is melted and mixture is smooth. Add sugar; bring to a boil. Boil for 2 to 3 minutes or until slightly thickened, stirring constantly. Remove from heat; stir in margarine and vanilla.

Orange-Chocolate Sauce: Prepare Regal Chocolate Sauce as directed, substituting 1 tablespoon orange liqueur for the vanilla.

Almond-Chocolate Sauce: Prepare Regal Chocolate Sauce as directed, substituting 1 tablespoon almond liqueur for the vanilla.

Mocha Sauce: Prepare Regal Chocolate Sauce as directed, adding 1 to 2 tablespoons instant coffee with sugar.

Cinnamon-Chocolate Sauce: Prepare Regal Chocolate Sauce as directed, adding ½ teaspoon cinnamon with sugar.

½ cup sugar

¼ cup HERSHEY'S Cocoa or
   HERSHEY'S European
   Style Cocoa

1 tablespoon plus 1 teaspoon
   cornstarch

½ cup evaporated skim milk

2 teaspoons vanilla extract
   Assorted fresh fruit, cut up
   (optional)
   Cake (optional)
   Nonfat frozen yogurt
   (optional)

SINFULLY RICH NONFAT FUDGE SAUCE

Makes 7 servings

In small saucepan, stir together sugar, cocoa and cornstarch; gradually stir in evaporated milk. Cook over low heat, stirring constantly with whisk, until mixture boils; continue cooking and stirring until thickened and smooth. Remove from heat; stir in vanilla. Serve warm or cold with assorted fresh fruit, cake or nonfat frozen yogurt, if desired. Cover; refrigerate leftover sauce.

C H O C O L A T E   T I P

Cocoa powder can be stored in an airtight container in a cool dark place for up to *two years. Never substitute cocoa mix for cocoa powder in a recipe.*

Sinfully Rich Nonfat Fudge Sauce

1 cup sugar

1 can (5 or 5⅓ ounces) evaporated milk

1 tablespoon light corn syrup

2 squares (1 ounce each) unsweetened chocolate or semi-sweet chocolate (for sweeter sauce)

3 tablespoons BUTTER FLAVOR* CRISCO® all-vegetable shortening

1 teaspoon finely grated orange peel

2 teaspoons orange-flavored liqueur or ½ teaspoon orange extract

¼ teaspoon salt

Butter Flavor Crisco is artificially flavored

CHOCOLATE–ORANGE DESSERT SAUCE

Makes 1½ cups

1. Combine sugar, evaporated milk and corn syrup in 1½- or 2-quart saucepan. Heat to a full boil over medium-high heat, stirring constantly. Boil for 1 minute, stirring constantly. Reduce heat to low; add chocolate and stir until smooth.

2. Remove from heat. Blend in shortening, orange peel, liqueur and salt. Serve warm over ice cream or cake.

Chocolate-Orange Dessert Sauce

⅔ cup KARO® Light or Dark
   Corn Syrup
½ cup heavy cream
8 squares (1 ounce each)
   semisweet chocolate
Assorted fresh fruit

CHOCOLATE PLUNGE

Makes 1½ cups

In medium saucepan combine corn syrup and cream. Bring to boil over medium heat. Remove from heat. Add chocolate; stir until completely melted. Serve warm as a dip for fruit.

PREP TIME: 10 MINUTES

Microwave Directions: In medium microwavable bowl combine corn syrup and cream. Microwave on HIGH (100%), 1½ minutes or until boiling. Add chocolate; stir until completely melted. Serve as above.

Note: Chocolate Plunge can be made a day ahead. Store covered in refrigerator. Reheat before serving.

TRY SOME OF THESE "DIPPERS:" Candied pineapple, dried apricots, waffle squares, lady fingers, macaroons, pretzels, croissants, mint cookies or peanut butter cookies.

Chocolate Plunge

2 cinnamon sticks

⅔ cup whipping cream

6 ounces white chocolate, chopped

¼ cup KAHLÚA®

Bite-size pieces of fruit, such as strawberries, raspberries, bananas, pineapple chunks, apple or orange wedges and cubes of pound cake or cookies

KAHLÚA® WHITE CHOCOLATE FONDUE

Makes 2 cups

Cut cinnamon sticks in half lengthwise; break each half into several pieces.

Combine cream and half of cinnamon pieces in small saucepan. Bring to a rolling boil; remove from heat. Cover and let stand 15 minutes. Add remaining cinnamon stick pieces; return to a boil. Remove from heat. Cover and let stand 15 minutes more.

Place white chocolate in medium bowl. Return cream to a boil once more; pour through strainer into bowl with white chocolate. Let stand 1 to 2 minutes; stir until smooth. Stir in Kahlúa®. Serve warm in fondue pot with bite-size pieces of fruit, cake or cookies.

30 HERSHEY'S KISSES® Milk Chocolates
½ cup HERSHEY'S Syrup
Any flavor ice cream

CHOCOLATE LOVER'S ICE CREAM SAUCE

Makes about 1 cup sauce

Remove wrappers from chocolate pieces. In small heavy saucepan combine syrup and chocolates. Stir constantly over very low heat until chocolates are melted and mixture is smooth; remove from heat. Spoon sauce over ice cream. Serve immediately. Cover and refrigerate leftover sauce.

TO REHEAT: In large bowl containing about 1 inch very hot water place smaller bowl containing sauce. Allow to stand several minutes to soften; stir to desired consistency.

Microwave Directions: In small microwave-safe bowl combine syrup and chocolates. Microwave on HIGH (100%) 15 seconds; stir well. Microwave additional 30 seconds; stir until chocolates are melted and mixture is smooth. If necessary, microwave additional 15 seconds or as needed to melt chocolates. To reheat refrigerated sauce, microwave on HIGH a few seconds at a time; stir. Repeat until warm.

⅔ cup nonfat dry milk powder

⅔ cup sugar

¼ cup HERSHEY'S Cocoa

2 tablespoons cornstarch

4 cups (1 quart) skim milk, divided

¼ teaspoon freshly grated orange peel

⅛ teaspoon orange extract

Orange Cups (optional, directions follow)

Additional freshly grated orange peel (optional)

TROPICAL CHOCOLATE ORANGE ICE MILK

Makes 8 servings

In medium saucepan, stir together milk powder, sugar, cocoa and cornstarch. Gradually stir in 2 cups skim milk. Cook over medium heat, stirring constantly, until mixture is smooth and slightly thickened, about 5 minutes. Remove from heat. Stir in remaining 2 cups milk, ¼ teaspoon orange peel and orange extract. Cover; refrigerate several hours until cold.

Pour mixture into 2-quart ice cream freezer container. Freeze according to manufacturer's directions. Place in freezer 6 hours or overnight. Before serving, let stand at room temperature until slightly softened. Scoop ½ cup ice milk into each Orange Cup or 8 individual dessert dishes. Garnish with additional orange peel, if desired.

ORANGE CUPS: Cut about 1-inch slice from tops of 8 oranges; discard. Using sharp knife, cut out and remove small triangle shaped notches around tops of oranges to make zig-zag pattern. Scoop out pulp; reserve for other uses.

Tropical Chocolate Orange Ice Milk

1 ripe medium banana
1½ cups orange juice
1 cup (½ pint) half-and-half
½ cup sugar
¼ cup HERSHEY'S Cocoa

REFRESHING COCOA–FRUIT SHERBET

Makes 8 servings

Into blender container, slice banana. Add orange juice; cover and blend until smooth. Add remaining ingredients; cover and blend well. Pour into 8- or 9-inch square pan. Cover; freeze until hard around edges.

Into blender container or large mixer bowl, spoon partially frozen mixture. Cover; blend until smooth but not melted. Pour into 1-quart mold. Cover; freeze until firm. Unmold onto cold plate and slice. Garnish as desired.

Variation: Add 2 teaspoons orange-flavored liqueur with orange juice.

CHOCOLATE TIP

As chocolate took a powerful hold on the candy and confections market, cocoa powder mixed with sugar and milk and served as a hot beverage became a popular wintertime drink. It wasn't until after World War II that powdered chocolate was processed so it would dissolve easily in cold milk providing a refreshing option for chocolate lovers—chocolate milk.

Refreshing Cocoa-Fruit Sherbet

2 ripe medium bananas
1 cup apricot nectar or peach or
    pineapple juice, divided
½ cup HERSHEY'S Semi-Sweet
    Chocolate Chips
2 tablespoons sugar
1 cup lowfat 2% milk

CHOCOLATE–BANANA SHERBET

Makes 8 servings

Into blender container or food processor, slice bananas. Add ¾ cup fruit juice. Cover; blend until smooth. In small microwave-safe bowl, place chocolate chips, remaining ¼ cup fruit juice and sugar. Microwave at HIGH (100%) 30 seconds; stir. If necessary, microwave at HIGH an additional 15 seconds at a time, stirring after each heating, just until chips are melted and mixture is smooth when stirred. Add to mixture in blender. Cover; blend until thoroughly combined. Add milk. Cover; blend until smooth. Pour into 8- or 9-inch square pan. Cover; freeze until hard around edges, about 2 hours.

In large mixer bowl or food processor, spoon partially frozen mixture; beat until smooth but not melted. Return mixture to pan. Cover; freeze until firm, stirring several times before mixture freezes. Before serving, let stand at room temperature 10 to 15 minutes until slightly softened. Scoop into 8 individual dessert dishes.

Chocolate-Banana Sherbet

BANANA ROCKY ROAD ICE CREAM

Makes 12 servings (about 1½ quarts)

3 extra-ripe, medium DOLE®
    Bananas, peeled
4 eggs
2 cups heavy or whipping cream
1 cup half-and-half
¾ cup sugar
1 teaspoon vanilla extract
4 squares (1 ounce each) semi-
    sweet chocolate
1 cup coarsely chopped walnuts
1 cup mini-marshmallows

■ Place bananas in food processor or blender. Process until smooth. Add eggs; process until blended. Pour banana mixture, cream, half-and-half, sugar and vanilla into freezer container of ice cream maker. Stir to dissolve sugar.

■ Melt chocolate in small bowl over hot water. Stir melted chocolate into banana mixture until blended. Freeze according to manufacturer's instructions.

■ While ice cream is still soft, stir in walnuts and marshmallows. Freeze until firm.

CHOCOLATE–AMARETTO ICE

Makes about 4 servings

¾ cup sugar
½ cup HERSHEY'S Cocoa
2 cups (1 pint) light cream or
    half-and-half
2 tablespoons Amaretto
    (almond-flavored) liqueur
Sliced almonds (optional)

In small saucepan, stir together sugar and cocoa; gradually stir in light cream. Cook over low heat, stirring constantly, until sugar dissolves and mixture is smooth and hot; do not boil. Remove from heat; stir in liqueur. Pour into 8-inch square pan. Cover; freeze until firm, stirring several times before mixture freezes. Scoop into dessert dishes. Serve frozen. Garnish with sliced almonds, if desired.

WHITE CHOCOLATE ICE CREAM

Makes 1 quart

1 cup BLUE DIAMOND® Whole Natural Almonds, coarsely chopped

1 tablespoon butter

3 cups whipping cream

1 cup milk

4 egg yolks

¾ cup sugar

1 tablespoon vanilla extract

½ cup kirsch

1 cup grated white chocolate

Sauté almonds in butter in skillet over medium heat until crisp; reserve. Combine cream and milk in saucepan; cook over medium heat until skin forms on surface. Beat yolks and sugar with vanilla in medium bowl; gradually add cream mixture, whisking constantly. Strain into double boiler and cook over simmering water, stirring, until mixture thickens and lightly coats the back of a spoon, about 10 minutes. *Do not boil.* Remove from heat; add kirsch and white chocolate, stirring until chocolate melts. Cool to room temperature. Add almonds. Pour into ice cream freezer container. Freeze according to manufacturer's instructions.

CHOCOLATE TIP

To grate chocolate, rub a chocolate square across the rough surface of a bell or hand-held grater. Use the side with large holes for larger pieces and the side with small holes for smaller pieces. Grated chocolate is an easy and beautiful garnish to any dessert.

1 cup all-purpose flour

¾ cup granulated sugar

½ cup unsweetened cocoa
   powder, divided

2 teaspoons baking powder

½ teaspoon salt

½ cup skim milk

¼ cup MOTT'S® Natural Apple
   Sauce

1 teaspoon vanilla extract

1¾ cups hot water

¾ cup firmly packed light brown
   sugar

½ gallon frozen nonfat vanilla
   yogurt
   Maraschino cherries
   (optional)

FUDGE BROWNIE SUNDAES

Makes 12 servings

1. Preheat oven to 350°F. Spray 8-inch square baking pan with nonstick cooking spray.

2. In large bowl, combine flour, granulated sugar, ¼ cup cocoa, baking powder and salt. Add milk, apple sauce and vanilla; stir until well blended. Pour batter into prepared pan.

3. In medium bowl, combine hot water, brown sugar and remaining ¼ cup cocoa. Pour over batter. *Do not stir.*

4. Bake 40 minutes or until center is almost set. Cool completely on wire rack. Cut into 12 bars. Top each bar with ½-cup scoop of frozen yogurt; spoon sauce from bottom of pan over yogurt. Garnish with cherry, if desired.

Fudge Brownie Sundaes

8 squares (1 ounce each)
semisweet chocolate
⅔ cup KARO® Light or Dark
Corn Syrup
2 cups heavy cream, divided
1½ cups broken cookies
(chocolate wafers or other
crisp cookies)
1 cup coarsely chopped walnuts
Chocolate, nuts and whipped
cream (optional)

CHOCOLATE TORTONI

Makes 12 servings

Line 12 (2½-inch) muffin pan cups with paper or foil liners. In large heavy saucepan combine chocolate and corn syrup; stir over low heat just until chocolate melts. Remove from heat. Stir in ½ cup of the cream until blended. Refrigerate 25 to 30 minutes or until cool. Stir in cookies and walnuts. In small bowl with mixer at medium speed, beat remaining 1½ cups cream until soft peaks form; gently fold into chocolate mixture just until combined. Spoon into prepared muffin pan cups. Freeze 4 to 6 hours or until firm. Let stand at room temperature several minutes before serving. If desired, garnish with chocolate, nuts or whipped cream. Store covered in freezer for up to 1 month.

PREP TIME: 15 MINUTES, PLUS CHILLING AND FREEZING

Microwave Directions: Prepare muffin pan cups as above. In 3-quart microwavable bowl combine chocolate and corn syrup. Microwave on HIGH (100%), 1 minute; stir. Microwave 1 to 1½ minutes; stir until smooth. Continue as above.

TORTONI SQUARES: Spread mixture in 9-inch square pan. Freeze as above. Let stand; cut into 9 squares.

Note: Granola, crunchy breakfast cereal or trail mix may be substituted for cookies or nuts in this quick-to-fix recipe. For more sophisticated flavor, use 8 ounces of imported mocha-flavored chocolate or try white chocolate for a completely different look and taste.

Chocolate Tortoni

2 pints chocolate chip ice cream, softened
1 package DUNCAN HINES® Moist Deluxe Dark Chocolate Fudge Cake Mix
½ cup butter or margarine, softened

ICE CREAM COOKIE SANDWICH

Makes 10 to 12 servings

1. Line bottom of one 9-inch round cake pan with aluminum foil. Spread ice cream in pan. Return to freezer until firm. Run knife around edge of pan to loosen ice cream. Remove from pan. Wrap in foil and return to freezer.

2. Preheat oven to 350°F. Line bottom of two 9-inch round cake pans with aluminum foil. Place cake mix in large bowl. Add butter. Mix until crumbs form. Place half the cake mix in each pan. Press lightly. Bake at 350°F for 15 minutes or until browned around edges; do not overbake. Cool 10 minutes. Remove from pans. Remove foil from cookie layers. Cool completely.

3. To assemble, place cookie layer on serving plate. Top with ice cream. Peel off foil. Place second cookie layer on top. Wrap in foil and freeze 2 hours. To keep longer, store in airtight container.

TIP: You can use lemon sherbet and Duncan Hines Moist Deluxe Lemon Supreme Cake Mix in place of chocolate chip ice cream and Moist Deluxe Dark Chocolate Fudge Cake Mix.

Ice Cream Cookie Sandwich

**Low Fat Devil's Chocolate
Fudge Cake (page 188)**
**1 quart fat free strawberry ice
cream or frozen yogurt**
4 egg whites
1¼ cups sugar
1 teaspoon vanilla
Dash of salt

NEAPOLITAN BAKED ALASKA

Makes 8 servings

Prepare Low Fat Devil's Chocolate Fudge Cake as directed, omitting icing. When cool, cut cake in half, each half measuring about 9×4½ inches. Reserve one half for another use. Place remaining cake half on double thickness of foil. Quickly mound ice cream on cake. Immediately place in freezer.* Fifteen minutes before serving, preheat oven to 500°F. To make meringue, in mixer bowl, beat egg whites at high speed until soft peaks form. Gradually add sugar, vanilla and salt, continuing to beat until stiff peaks form. Transfer cake and ice cream to ovenproof platter or board using foil. Quickly cover cake and ice cream completely with meringue; swirl meringue with back of spoon. Bake in center of oven about 5 to 7 minutes just until meringue is lightly browned. Slice and serve immediately.

After ice cream is solidly frozen, cake and ice cream can be wrapped in plastic or foil and stored in freezer for up to 2 weeks.

TIP: The secret to a successful Baked Alaska is to completely cover solidly frozen ice cream and cake with meringue, which acts as an insulating blanket when the Baked Alaska is popped into a hot oven for browning.

FAVORITE RECIPE FROM CALIFORNIA PRUNE BOARD

Neapolitan Baked Alaska

Low Fat Devil's Chocolate Fudge Cake (page 188)

1 pint vanilla fat free frozen yogurt

2½ cups chocolate fat free frozen yogurt

3 cups strawberry fat free frozen yogurt

Fruit purée (recipe follows)

FROZEN CHOCOLATE YOGURT BOMBE

Makes 12 servings

Prepare Low Fat Devil's Chocolate Fudge Cake batter as directed, omitting icing, but spread into nonstick jelly-roll pan coated with vegetable cooking spray. Bake at 350°F for about 20 minutes or until pick inserted into center comes out clean. Cool in pan on wire rack 10 minutes; invert onto rack. Cool completely. Line 2½-quart stainless steel bowl with plastic wrap, smoothing surface to avoid wrinkles. Cut cake into 4-inch-wide strips. Line bowl with strips of cake, cutting and piecing together to avoid gaps; reserve remaining cake. Freeze cake in bowl 15 minutes. Meanwhile, soften vanilla yogurt; spread in cake-lined bowl, smoothing surface. Freeze 15 minutes or until top feels firm. Meanwhile, soften chocolate yogurt. Spread over vanilla layer, smoothing surface; return to freezer for 15 minutes. Meanwhile, soften strawberry yogurt. Spread over chocolate yogurt. Top with remaining cake strips, cutting strips as needed to completely cover. Cover tightly with plastic wrap; freeze at least 4 hours. Remove from freezer 30 minutes before serving. Meanwhile, prepare Fruit Purée. To serve, cut bombe into wedges. Spoon ¼ cup Fruit Purée onto each serving plate. Top with bombe.

FRUIT PURÉE: Process enough fresh berries, peeled peaches or apricots in food processor to measure 3 cups.

FAVORITE RECIPE FROM **CALIFORNIA PRUNE BOARD**

1 tub (8 ounces) COOL WHIP®
    Whipped Topping, thawed
⅓ cup chopped pecans, divided
1 cup half-and-half or milk
1 package (4-serving size)
    JELL-O® Chocolate Flavor
    Instant Pudding & Pie
    Filling
2 bars (1.4 ounces each)
    chocolate-covered English
    toffee, chopped (about
    ½ cup)
Additional chopped pecans
Additional chopped
    chocolate-covered English
    toffee

CHOCOLATE CRUNCH BOMBE

Makes 6 to 8 servings

RESERVE ½ cup of the whipped topping for garnish; refrigerate.

SPOON remaining whipped topping into medium bowl; set aside. Rinse and dry tub; spray with no stick cooking spray. Place 2 tablespoons pecans in bottom of tub.

POUR half-and-half into large bowl. Add pudding mix. Beat with wire whisk 2 minutes. Gently stir in 2 cups of the whipped topping. Spoon ½ of the pudding mixture over pecans in tub.

MIX remaining pecans and chopped toffee bars into remaining whipped topping in medium bowl. Spread over pudding mixture in tub. Top with remaining pudding mixture. Cover with plastic wrap.

FREEZE 6 hours or overnight. To unmold, run warm wet metal spatula around edge of tub. Place serving dish on top of tub. Invert, holding tub and dish together; shake gently to loosen. Carefully remove tub. Garnish with reserved ½ cup whipped topping, additional chopped pecans and toffee candy. Cut into slices to serve.

TUB TIPS: For a pretty serving dish, use scissors to scallop the edge of any size clean COOL WHIP® tub, then glue ribbons and soft fabric to cover outside of tub. Fill with small candies or cookies.

½ cup granulated sugar

2 tablespoons cornstarch

3 egg yolks

1 cup milk

3 bars (6 ounces) NESTLÉ®
    Unsweetened Baking
    Chocolate, broken up

3 tablespoons almond liqueur

48 (two 3-ounce packages)
    ladyfingers, halved

1½ cups heavy whipping cream

1 cup powdered sugar
    Sweetened whipped cream
    (optional)
    Chocolate Curls (optional)

CHOCOLATE DELIGHT

Makes 10 servings

COMBINE sugar and cornstarch in 2-quart saucepan. Whisk in egg yolks and milk. Cook over medium-low heat, stirring constantly with wire whisk until mixture boils; boil for 1 minute, whisking constantly. Remove from heat. Add baking bars; whisk until mixture is smooth. Whisk in liqueur. Press plastic wrap directly on surface of chocolate mixture. Cool to room temperature.

LINE side of 9-inch springform pan with ladyfingers, cut sides in. Arrange half of remaining ladyfingers on bottom of pan.

BEAT cream and powdered sugar in small mixer bowl until stiff peaks form. Stir chocolate mixture until smooth; fold in whipped cream. Spoon half of chocolate mixture into pan. Layer with remaining ladyfingers and chocolate mixture. Cover; chill for 4 hours or overnight. Remove rim; garnish with whipped cream and chocolate curls.

Chocolate Delight

27 whole graham crackers,
   halved
3 cups cold milk
2 packages (4-serving size)
   JELL-O® Vanilla Flavor
   Instant Pudding & Pie
   Filling
1 tub (12 ounces) COOL WHIP®
   Whipped Topping, thawed
1 container (16 ounces) ready-
   to-spread chocolate fudge
   frosting
   Strawberries

EASY ECLAIR DESSERT
Makes 18 servings

ARRANGE ⅓ of the crackers on bottom of 13×9-inch baking pan, breaking crackers to fit, if necessary.

POUR milk into large bowl. Add pudding mixes. Beat with wire whisk 2 minutes. Gently stir in whipped topping. Spread ½ of the pudding mixture over crackers. Place ½ of the remaining crackers over pudding; top with remaining pudding mixture and crackers.

REMOVE top and foil from frosting container. Microwave frosting in container on HIGH 1 minute or until pourable. Spread evenly over crackers.

REFRIGERATE 4 hours or overnight. Cut into squares to serve. Garnish with strawberries.

COOL TIPS: You can make pistachio, banana-flavored or even double chocolate eclairs by simply changing the pudding flavors.

Easy Eclair Dessert

1 package DUNCAN HINES®
    Double Fudge Brownie Mix
2 eggs
⅓ cup water
¼ cup CRISCO® Oil or CRISCO®
    PURITAN® Canola Oil
½ gallon raspberry sherbet,
    softened
1 package (12 ounces) frozen
    dry pack red raspberries,
    thawed and undrained
⅓ cup sugar
    Fresh raspberries, for garnish

RASPBERRY SHERBET BROWNIE DESSERT

Makes 12 to 16 servings

1. Preheat oven to 350°F. Grease bottom of 13×9×2-inch pan.

2. Combine brownie mix, contents of fudge packet from mix, eggs, water and oil in large bowl. Stir with spoon until well blended, about 50 strokes. Spread in pan. Bake and cool brownies following package directions. Spread softened sherbet over cooled brownies. Cover and freeze for 3 to 4 hours or overnight until firm.

3. For raspberry sauce, combine thawed raspberries with juice and sugar in small saucepan. Bring to a boil. Simmer until berries are soft. Push mixture through sieve into small bowl to remove seeds. Cool completely.

4. To serve, cut dessert into squares. Spoon raspberry sauce over each serving. Garnish with fresh raspberries.

TIP: Raspberries are most plentiful during June and July. They should be plump with a hollow core. Plan to use them within 1 or 2 days after purchase.

Raspberry Sherbet Brownie Dessert

½ cup KARO® Light or Dark
   Corn Syrup

⅓ cup evaporated milk

3 cups (18 ounces) semisweet
   chocolate chips

¾ cup confectioners' sugar,
   sifted

2 teaspoons vanilla

1 cup coarsely chopped nuts
   (optional)

FAST 'N' FABULOUS DARK CHOCOLATE FUDGE

Makes 25 squares

Line 8-inch square baking pan with plastic wrap. In 3-quart microwavable bowl, combine corn syrup and evaporated milk; stir until well blended. Microwave on HIGH (100%), 3 minutes. Stir in chocolate chips until melted. Stir in confectioners' sugar, vanilla and nuts. With wooden spoon beat until thick and glossy. Spread in prepared pan. Refrigerate 2 hours or until firm.

PREP TIME: 10 MINUTES, PLUS CHILLING

MARVELOUS MARBLE FUDGE: Omit nuts. Prepare as directed above; spread into prepared pan. Drop ⅓ cup Skippy® creamy peanut butter over fudge in small dollops. With small spatula, swirl fudge to marbleize. Continue as above.

DOUBLE PEANUT BUTTER CHOCOLATE FUDGE: Prepare as directed above. Stir in ⅓ cup Skippy® Super Chunk® peanut butter. Spread in prepared pan. Drop additional ⅓ cup peanut butter over fudge in small dollops. With small spatula, swirl fudge to marbleize. Continue as above.

Fast 'n' Fabulous Dark Chocolate Fudge

1 package (8 ounces) BAKER'S®
  Semi-Sweet Chocolate
⅔ cup sweetened condensed
  milk
1 teaspoon vanilla
⅛ teaspoon salt
½ cup chopped nuts (optional)

ONE BOWL® CHOCOLATE FUDGE

Makes about 2 dozen candies

MICROWAVE chocolate and milk in 1½-quart microwavable bowl on HIGH 1 minute; stir well. Microwave 1 minute longer. **Stir until chocolate is completely melted and smooth.** Stir in vanilla, salt and nuts. Spread into greased 8×4- or 9×5-inch loaf pan. Refrigerate until firm; cut into squares.

SAUCEPAN PREPARATION: Heat chocolate and milk in 2-quart saucepan over very low heat, stirring constantly, until chocolate is melted and mixture is smooth. Remove from heat. Continue as above.

PEANUT BUTTER FUDGE

PREPARE ONE BOWL® Chocolate Fudge and spread into pan as directed. Immediately drop ¼ cup peanut butter by rounded spoonfuls on top of fudge. Swirl peanut butter through fudge with knife to marbleize. Refrigerate and cut into squares. *Makes about 2 dozen candies*

ROCKY ROAD FUDGE

PREPARE ONE BOWL® Chocolate Fudge as directed, adding 1 cup KRAFT® Miniature Marshmallows to fudge with the vanilla, salt and nuts. Refrigerate and cut into squares. *Makes about 2 dozen candies*

PREP TIME: 10 MINUTES
CHILL TIME: 30 MINUTES

Clockwise from top right: Rocky Road Fudge, Peanut Butter Fudge and ONE BOWL® Chocolate Fudge

1 can (12 ounces) evaporated
   milk
2 cups (11½ ounces) milk
   chocolate chips
1 cup (6 ounces) semisweet
   chocolate chips
1 jar (7 ounces) marshmallow
   creme
¼ cup butter or margarine
4 cups sugar
   Dash salt
1 teaspoon vanilla
2½ to 3 cups chopped pecans,
   divided

DOUBLE CHOCOLATE–CREME FUDGE

Makes about 4 pounds

Butter 13×9-inch pan; set aside. Lightly butter side of heavy large saucepan.

Combine evaporated milk, chips, marshmallow creme, butter, sugar and salt in prepared saucepan. Cook over medium heat, stirring constantly, until sugar dissolves and mixture comes to a boil. Wash down side of pan with pastry brush frequently dipped in hot water to remove sugar crystals.

Add candy thermometer. Stir mixture occasionally. Continue to cook until mixture reaches soft-ball stage (238°F). Pour into large heatproof mixer bowl. Cool to lukewarm. Add vanilla and beat with heavy-duty electric mixer until thick. Beat in 1 cup chopped pecans when candy starts to lose its gloss. Immediately spread into prepared pan. Sprinkle remaining chopped pecans over fudge; gently press into fudge. Score fudge into squares. Refrigerate until firm. Cut into squares. Refrigerate.

4 cups sugar

1 jar (7 ounces) marshmallow
creme

1½ cups (12-ounce can)
evaporated milk

1 tablespoon butter or
margarine

4 cups (24-ounce package)
HERSHEY₂S Semi-Sweet
Chocolate Chips

SEMI-SWEET CHOCOLATE FUDGE

Makes about 8 dozen squares

Line 13×9×2-inch pan with foil extending over edges of pan. Butter foil lightly. In heavy 4-quart saucepan, stir together sugar, marshmallow creme, evaporated milk and butter. Cook over medium heat, stirring constantly, until mixture comes to a full rolling boil; boil and stir 5 minutes. Remove from heat; immediately add chocolate chips, stirring until smooth. Pour into prepared pan; cool until firm. Using foil to lift fudge out of pan, remove. Peel off foil. Cut into squares. Store in airtight container in cool, dry place.

CHOCOLATE TIP

The rich creamy chocolate confection we call fudge has been around for over 100 years. It was first made in women's colleges in England, where candy making was often used as an excuse to stay up late.

1 cup REESE₂S Peanut Butter
   Chips
1 cup HERSHEY₂S Semi-Sweet
   Chocolate Chips or
   HERSHEY₂S MINI CHIPS®
   Semi-Sweet Chocolate
2¼ cups sugar
1 jar (7 ounces) marshmallow
   creme
¾ cup evaporated milk
¼ cup (½ stick) butter or
   margarine
1 teaspoon vanilla extract

DOUBLE–DECKER FUDGE

Makes 5 dozen pieces or about 2 pounds fudge

Line 8-inch square pan with foil, extending foil over edges of pan. In medium bowl, place peanut butter chips. In second medium bowl, place chocolate chips. In heavy 3-quart saucepan, combine sugar, marshmallow creme, evaporated milk and butter. Cook over medium heat, stirring constantly, until mixture comes to a boil; boil 5 minutes, stirring constantly. Remove from heat; stir in vanilla. Immediately stir half of the hot mixture (1½ cups) into peanut butter chips until chips are completely melted; quickly spread into prepared pan. Stir remaining hot mixture into chocolate chips until chips are completely melted. Quickly spread over top of peanut butter layer. Cool to room temperature; refrigerate until firm. Use foil to lift fudge out of pan; peel off foil. Cut into 1-inch squares. Store tightly covered in refrigerator.

PEANUT BUTTER FUDGE: Omit chocolate chips; place 1⅔ cups (10-ounce package) REESE₂S Peanut Butter Chips in large bowl. Cook fudge mixture as directed; add to chips, stirring until chips are completely melted. Pour into prepared pan.

CHOCOLATE FUDGE: Omit peanut butter chips; place 2 cups (12-ounce package) HERSHEY₂S Semi-Sweet Chocolate Chips in large bowl. Cook fudge mixture as directed; add to chips, stirring until chips are completely melted. Pour into prepared pan.

From top to bottom: Semi-Sweet Chocolate Fudge (page 353) and Double-Decker Fudge

1 cup (2 sticks) butter or
    margarine

1 cup sugar

3 tablespoons water

1 tablespoon corn syrup

½ cup toasted chopped almonds

6 squares BAKER'S® Semi-Sweet
    Chocolate, melted

⅓ cup toasted finely chopped
    almonds

CHOCOLATE–COATED ALMOND TOFFEE

Makes about 1½ pounds candy

COOK butter, sugar, water and corn syrup in heavy 2-quart saucepan over medium heat until mixture boils, stirring constantly. Boil gently, stirring frequently, 10 to 12 minutes or until golden brown and very thick. (Or until ½ teaspoon of mixture will form a hard, brittle thread when dropped in 1 cup cold water.)

REMOVE from heat. Stir in ½ cup almonds. Spread evenly into well-buttered 15½×10½×1-inch baking pan. Let stand until almost cool to the touch.

SPREAD melted chocolate over toffee; sprinkle with ⅓ cup almonds. Let stand until chocolate is firm. Break into pieces.

PREP TIME: 30 MINUTES

*From left to right : Easy Chocolate Truffles
(page 358) and Chocolate-Coated Almond Toffee*

1 package (8 ounces)
  PHILADELPHIA BRAND®
  Cream Cheese, softened
3 cups powdered sugar
1½ packages (12 ounces)
  BAKER'S® Semi-Sweet
  Chocolate, melted
1½ teaspoons vanilla
  Ground nuts, unsweetened
    cocoa or BAKER'S® ANGEL
    FLAKE® Coconut, toasted

EASY CHOCOLATE TRUFFLES

Makes about 5 dozen candies

BEAT cream cheese until smooth. Gradually add sugar, beating until well blended. Add melted chocolate and vanilla; mix well. Refrigerate about 1 hour. Shape into 1-inch balls. Roll in nuts, cocoa or coconut. Store in refrigerator.

PREP TIME: 15 MINUTES

CHILL TIME: 1 HOUR

Variation: *To flavor truffles with liqueurs, omit vanilla. Divide truffle mixture into thirds. Add 1 tablespoon liqueur (almond, coffee or orange) to each third mixture; mix well.*

---

1 cup heavy cream
16 ounces semisweet chocolate,
  cut into small pieces
2 tablespoons butter
1 cup finely chopped walnuts
4 tablespoons coffee liqueur
  Grated chocolate, shredded
    coconut and finely chopped
    walnuts

CHOCOLATE WALNUT TRUFFLES

Makes 3½ dozen truffles

Bring heavy cream to a boil in large saucepan over medium heat; add chocolate. Stir with wooden spoon until mixture is smooth and thick; stir in butter. Pour into large bowl; cool. Stir in walnuts and liqueur; refrigerate until firm. Form into 1-inch balls and roll in chocolate, coconut or walnuts; refrigerate until set. Store in airtight container in refrigerator.

FAVORITE RECIPE FROM **WALNUT MARKETING BOARD**

6 squares BAKER'S® Semi-Sweet
    Chocolate
¼ cup (½ stick) PARKAY®
    Margarine
2⅔ cups (7 ounces) BAKER'S®
    ANGEL FLAKE® Coconut
1 package (8 ounces)
    PHILADELPHIA BRAND®
    Cream Cheese, softened
2½ cups cold half and half or milk
1 package (6-serving size)
    JELL-O® Chocolate Flavor
    Instant Pudding & Pie
    Filling
2 tablespoons unsweetened
    cocoa
1 tablespoon confectioners'
    sugar

TRUFFLE TREATS

Makes about 20 pieces

PLACE chocolate in heavy saucepan over very low heat; stir constantly until just melted. Remove 2 tablespoons of the melted chocolate; set aside.

STIR margarine into remaining chocolate in saucepan until melted. Gradually stir in coconut, tossing to coat evenly. Press mixture into 13×9-inch baking pan which has been lined with foil.

BEAT cream cheese at medium speed of electric mixer until smooth; beat in reserved 2 tablespoons chocolate. Gradually mix in half and half. Add pudding mix. Beat at low speed until well blended, about 1 minute. Pour over crust. Freeze until firm, about 4 hours or overnight.

MIX together cocoa and sugar in small bowl; sift over truffle mixture. Lift with foil from pan onto cutting board; let stand 10 minutes to soften slightly. Cut into diamonds, squares or triangles.

PREP TIME: 15 MINUTES
FREEZE TIME: 4 HOURS

DARK CHOCOLATE TRUFFLES

1⅔ cups chopped semisweet
   chocolate or semisweet
   chocolate chips
6 tablespoons whipping cream*
1 tablespoon cold butter or
   margarine, cut into pieces
1 teaspoon vanilla
½ cup chopped macadamia nuts
   or toffee, or chocolate
   decors

*To flavor with liqueur, reduce cream
to ¼ cup. Stir 2 tablespoons liqueur
into chocolate mixture along with
vanilla.

TRUFFLES

Makes 18 truffles

1. Place chocolate in small bowl. Combine whipping cream and butter in small saucepan. Simmer over medium-high heat until butter melts, stirring constantly with wooden spoon. Pour over chocolate; stir once.

2. Cover bowl; let stand 3 to 5 minutes. Uncover; stir until chocolate is melted and mixture is smooth. Stir in vanilla and liqueur, if using. Cover. Refrigerate 15 minutes or until mixture is firm enough to hold its shape.

3. Place level tablespoonfuls mixture on plate. Cover; refrigerate 2 hours or until fudgy, but not soft.

4. Place nuts in medium bowl. To make Truffles, roll each tablespoon chocolate mixture into ball. Roll Truffles in coating to evenly coat. (Warm hands and room temperature quickly soften chocolate, making it difficult to form balls. Keeping chocolate chilled prevents sticking.)

5. Store tightly covered in refrigerator up to 3 weeks. Serve chilled or let stand at room temperature 15 to 20 minutes before serving.

continued on page 362

Truffles

Truffles continued from page 360

WHITE CHOCOLATE TRUFFLES

1⅔ cups (10 ounces) chopped white chocolate or white chocolate chips

¼ cup whipping cream*

½ teaspoon vanilla

½ cup chopped macadamia nuts or toffee, or chocolate decors

1. Place chocolate in small bowl. Place whipping cream in small saucepan. Simmer over medium-high heat until heated through, stirring constantly with wooden spoon. Pour over chocolate, stir once.

2. Cover bowl; let stand 3 to 5 minutes. Uncover; stir until chocolate is melted and mixture is smooth. Stir in vanilla and liqueur, if using. Cover. Refrigerate 15 minutes or until mixture is firm enough to hold its shape.

3. Shape and coat truffles as directed in Steps 3 to 5 on page 360.   *Makes 18 truffles*

To flavor with liqueur, reduce cream to 2 tablespoons. Stir 2 tablespoons hazelnut- or almond-flavored liqueur into chocolate mixture along with vanilla.

GIANDUIA TRUFFLES

6 tablespoons butter or margarine*

6 ounces (1 cup) chopped milk chocolate or milk chocolate chips

1 cup toasted hazelnuts or unblanched almonds

½ cup chopped macadamia nuts or toffee, or chocolate decors

1. Melt butter in small saucepan over low heat, stirring occasionally with wooden spoon.

2. Remove saucepan from heat. Add chocolate; stir until melted. Stir in nuts. Refrigerate 15 minutes or until firm.

3. Shape and coat truffles as directed in Steps 3 to 5 on page 360.

Makes 18 truffles

*To flavor with liqueur, reduce butter to 2 tablespoons. Stir 2 tablespoons hazelnut- or almond-flavored liqueur into melted chocolate mixture.

C H O C O L A T E   T I P

Before chocolate became a taste sensation around the world, the cocoa bean had other valuable uses.

In A.D. 1000, the people of Central America used cocoa beans as a form of payment.

4 to 5 small apples
Wooden sticks
1 package (7 ounces) Chocolate
    RIESEN® Caramels
¼ cup heavy or whipping cream
1 cup coarsely chopped roasted
    cashews, pecans or peanuts

GOURMET CHOCOLATE/CARAMEL APPLES

Makes 4 to 5 servings

Wash and dry apples. Insert stick into stem end of each apple. Set aside. In a small heavy saucepan, combine caramels and cream. Heat over low heat, stirring frequently, until smooth. Dip each apple into the hot sauce, turning to coat. If sauce is too hot to coat well, let stand several minutes and dip again. Scrape excess sauce from bottom of each apple; roll bottom and halfway up sides of each apple in nuts. Place on greased wax paper. Chill until ready to serve. Allow to stand at room temperature several minutes before serving.

Microwave Directions: *Place candies and cream in small deep glass bowl. Microwave at 30% power 2 to 4 minutes, stirring well after each minute of cooking. Sauce will appear to be lumpy but after stirring will become smooth and shiny. Be careful not to overcook. Continue as above.*

Gourmet Chocolate/Caramel Apples

2 ripe medium bananas

4 wooden sticks

½ cup low fat granola cereal without raisins

⅓ cup hot fudge sauce, at room temperature

FROZEN CHOCOLATE–COVERED BANANAS

Makes 4 servings

1. Cover baking sheet or 15×10-inch jelly-roll pan with waxed paper; set aside.

2. Peel bananas; cut each in half crosswise. Insert wooden stick into center of cut end of each banana about 1½ inches into banana half. Place on prepared baking sheet; freeze until firm, at least 2 hours.

3. Place granola in large plastic food storage bag; crush slightly using rolling pin or meat mallet. Transfer granola to shallow plate. Place fudge sauce in a shallow dish.

4. Working with 1 banana at a time, place frozen banana in fudge sauce; turn banana and spread fudge sauce evenly onto banana with small rubber scraper. Immediately place banana on plate with granola; turn to coat lightly. Return to baking sheet in freezer. Repeat with remaining bananas.

5. Freeze until fudge sauce is very firm, at least 2 hours. Place on small plates; let stand 5 minutes before serving.

Frozen Chocolate-Covered Bananas

1 cup chopped toasted almonds

1⅔ cups (about 10 ounces) chopped white chocolate

2 cups (about 12 ounces) chopped semisweet chocolate

1⅔ cups (about 10 ounces) chopped milk chocolate

3 tablespoons shortening, divided

Heart-shaped pretzels

Biscotti

Chocolate sandwich cookies

Decorator Frosting (recipe follows)

Liquid food coloring

Ridged potato chips

EQUIPMENT:

Small paint brushes

CHOCOLATE–DIPPED DELIGHTS

Makes 3 cups melted chocolate

1. Place nuts in medium bowl. Set aside. To melt chocolate, place each chocolate and 1 tablespoon shortening in separate 4-cup glass measures. Microwave, 1 measure at a time, at MEDIUM (50% power) 4 to 5 minutes or until chocolate is melted, stirring after 2 minutes.

2. Place large sheet waxed paper on counter. Dip ½ of each pretzel into white chocolate. Gently shake off excess chocolate; place on waxed paper. Let stand 10 minutes; repeat. Let stand 30 minutes or until set.

3. Dip other halves of pretzels into semisweet chocolate. Place on waxed paper. Let stand until set.

4. Spread milk chocolate on curved edge of biscotti with small knife. Roll in nuts. Place on waxed paper. Let stand 30 minutes or until set.

5. Holding cookie flat, dip 1 side of each cookie into semisweet chocolate. Shake off excess chocolate. Place on waxed paper. Let stand 30 minutes or until set. Repeat with second side.

6. Prepare Decorator Frosting. Tint with liquid food coloring, if desired. Pipe design on cookies, if desired.

continued on page 370

Chocolate-Dipped Delights

Chocolate-Dipped Delights continued from page 368

7. To paint potato chips, dip paint brush into milk chocolate. Paint chocolate onto 1 side of each chip. Let stand 30 minutes or until set.

8. Store loosely covered at room temperature up to 1 week.

DECORATOR FROSTING

¾ **cup butter, softened**

4½ **cups powdered sugar, sifted**

3 **tablespoons water**

1 **teaspoon vanilla**

¼ **teaspoon lemon extract**

Beat butter in medium bowl with electric mixer at medium speed until smooth. Add 2 cups sugar. Beat at medium speed until light and fluffy. Add water and extracts. Beat at low speed until well blended, scraping down side of bowl once. Beat in remaining 2½ cups sugar until mixture is creamy.

Makes 2 cups

CHOCOLATE TIP

Occasionally chocolate may have white or grey streaks on the surface. This slight discoloration is called **bloom** *and is not a cause for worry. Bloom may occur when chocolate is stored at too high a temperature. High temperatures causes cocoa butter to separate, come to the surface and crystallize. The cocoa butter will recombine when the chocolate is melted and neither flavor or texture will be compromised.*

2 quarts popped JOLLY TIME®
  Pop Corn
15 graham cracker squares
 4 cups miniature
    marshmallows, divided
 1 cup semi-sweet chocolate
    pieces
 2 tablespoons butter or
    margarine

POP CORN S'MORES

Makes 15 s'mores

Preheat oven to 350°F. Put popped pop corn in large bowl. Arrange graham cracker squares in bottom of 13×9-inch baking pan; trim slightly if necessary to fit pan. Sprinkle with 2 cups marshmallows and chocolate pieces. Place butter in 2-quart glass measuring pitcher. Microwave at HIGH (100% power) until butter is melted, about 45 seconds. Stir in remaining 2 cups marshmallows until well coated. Microwave at HIGH (100% power) until marshmallows look puffy, about 1 minute; stir to melt completely. Pour marshmallow mixture over popped pop corn and mix well. Spread coated pop corn evenly over chocolate pieces in pan. Bake until marshmallows are puffy and appear to be melted, about 6 minutes. Invert pan onto cutting board and cut into squares between graham crackers.

ROCKY ROAD CLUSTERS

Makes about 2 dozen candies

2 cups (12-ounce package) NESTLÉ® TOLL HOUSE® Semi-Sweet Chocolate Morsels
1¼ cups (14-ounce can) CARNATION® Sweetened Condensed Milk
2½ cups miniature marshmallows
1 cup coarsely chopped nuts
1 teaspoon vanilla extract

COMBINE morsels and sweetened condensed milk in large microwave-safe bowl. Microwave on HIGH (100%) power for 1 minute; stir until smooth. If necessary, microwave for 20 to 30 seconds longer to complete melting. Stir in marshmallows, nuts and vanilla.

DROP by heaping tablespoonfuls into mounds on waxed paper. Chill until firm.

MOCHA–WALNUT RUM BALLS

Makes about 100 balls

1 package (8½ ounces) chocolate cookie wafers
2 cups powdered sugar, divided
1¼ cups finely chopped toasted walnuts
2 tablespoons instant coffee granules
⅓ to ½ cup rum
2 tablespoons light corn syrup
½ teaspoon instant espresso coffee powder

Process cookie wafers in food processor or blender to form powdery crumbs. Combine crumbs, 1½ cups sugar and walnuts in large bowl. Dissolve coffee granules in ⅓ cup rum; stir in corn syrup. Blend into crumb mixture until crumbs are moistened enough to hold together. Add 2 to 3 tablespoons more rum, if necessary. Shape into 1-inch balls. Mix remaining ½ cup sugar with espresso coffee powder. Roll balls in sugar mixture to coat. Store loosely packed between sheets of waxed paper or foil in airtight container up to 2 weeks.

Rocky Road Clusters

Acknowledgments

The publisher would like to thank the companies and organizations listed below for the use of their recipes and photographs in this publication.

Best Foods, a Division of CPC International Inc.

Blue Diamond Growers

California Prune Board

Dole Food Company, Inc.

Hershey Foods Corporation

Jolly Time® Pop Corn

Kahlúa Liqueur

Kellogg Company

Kraft Foods, Inc.

M&M/MARS

MOTT'S® Inc., a division of Cadbury Beverages Inc.

Nabisco, Inc.

Nestlé Food Company

The Procter & Gamble Company

The Quaker Oats Company

Ralston Foods, Inc.

Chocolate Riesen® Caramels

Sargento Foods Inc.®

The Sugar Association, Inc.

USA Rice Council

Walnut Marketing Board

Index

VOLUME MEASUREMENTS (dry)

1/8 teaspoon = 0.5 mL
1/4 teaspoon = 1 mL
1/2 teaspoon = 2 mL
3/4 teaspoon = 4 mL
1 teaspoon = 5 mL
1 tablespoon = 15 mL
2 tablespoons = 30 mL
1/4 cup = 60 mL
1/3 cup = 75 mL
1/2 cup = 125 mL
2/3 cup = 150 mL
3/4 cup = 175 mL
1 cup = 250 mL
2 cups = 1 pint = 500 mL
3 cups = 750 mL
4 cups = 1 quart = 1 L

VOLUME MEASUREMENTS (fluid)

1 fluid ounce (2 tablespoons) = 30 mL
4 fluid ounces (1/2 cup) = 125 mL
8 fluid ounces (1 cup) = 250 mL
12 fluid ounces (1 1/2 cups) = 375 mL
16 fluid ounces (2 cups) = 500 mL

WEIGHTS (mass)

1/2 ounce = 15 g
1 ounce = 30 g
3 ounces = 90 g
4 ounces = 120 g
8 ounces = 225 g
10 ounces = 285 g
12 ounces = 360 g
16 ounces = 1 pound = 450 g

DIMENSIONS

1/16 inch = 2 mm
1/8 inch = 3 mm
1/4 inch = 6 mm
1/2 inch = 1.5 cm
3/4 inch = 2 cm
1 inch = 2.5 cm

OVEN TEMPERATURES

250°F = 120°C
275°F = 140°C
300°F = 150°C
325°F = 160°C
350°F = 180°C
375°F = 190°C
400°F = 200°C
425°F = 220°C
450°F = 230°C

BAKING PAN SIZES

Utensil	Size in Inches/Quarts	Metric Volume	Size in Centimeters
Baking or Cake Pan (square or rectangular)	8×8×2	2 L	20×20×5
	9×9×2	2.5 L	22×22×5
	12×8×2	3 L	30×20×5
	13×9×2	3.5 L	33×23×5
Loaf Pan	8×4×3	1.5 L	20×10×7
	9×5×3	2 L	23×13×7
Round Layer Cake Pan	8×1½	1.2 L	20×4
	9×1½	1.5 L	23×4
Pie Plate	8×1¼	750 mL	20×3
	9×1¼	1 L	23×3
Baking Dish or Casserole	1 quart	1 L	—
	1½ quart	1.5 L	—
	2 quart	2 L	—